T0038729

Stressilient

HOW TO BEAT STRESS AND BUILD RESILIENCE

DR. SAM AKBAR

ST. MARTIN'S
ESSENTIALS
NEW YORK

Published in the United States by St. Martin's Essentials,
an imprint of St. Martin's Publishing Group

STRESSILIENT. Copyright © 2023 by Sam Akbar. All rights reserved.
Printed in the United States of America. For information, address
St. Martin's Publishing Group, 120 Broadway, New York, NY 10271.

www.stmartins.com

The Library of Congress Cataloging-in-Publication data is available upon request.

ISBN 978-1-250-88342-1 (trade paperback)
ISBN 978-1-250-88343-8 (ebook)

Our books may be purchased in bulk for promotional, educational, or business use.
Please contact your local bookseller or the Macmillan Corporate and
Premium Sales Department at 1-800-221-7945, extension 5442, or
by email at MacmillanSpecialMarkets@macmillan.com.

First published in the UK by 4th Estate, an imprint of HarperCollins Publishing in 2022

First St. Martin's Essentials Trade Paperback Edition: 2023

10 9 8 7 6 5 4 3 2 1

For Sophia, my wise one.

Contents

Contents

Introduction

I can't eliminate stress from your life.

I might as well say that upfront, so you don't feel wronged. I should also add that *no one else* can totally eliminate stress from your life either, unless they are proposing to cryogenically freeze you for the rest of your life, in which case, I hope you like the cold.

But here's what I can do (and it's better than stress elimination): I can teach you about *psychological flexibility*. Psychological flexibility is the ability to respond in a much more effective way to life's inevitable stresses and the emotions and thoughts these throw up. Building up resilience means taking action to live a life that is rewarding and meaningful—to become, in short, Stressilient.

This concept of psychological flexibility is at the heart of a groundbreaking and innovative therapeutic approach known as Acceptance and Commitment Therapy (ACT).

Over the last four decades, ACT has been shown to be effective not just in treating serious mental health conditions, such as depression and anxiety, but also with relationships, weight loss, smoking cessation, enhanced performance and stress management. ACT is an approach you can apply across the board from improving your relationship with your partner or managing a toxic boss to becoming healthier or coping with chronic stress.

And I don't know about you, but I'd say the last two years have been stressful, what with the MASSIVE GLOBAL PANDEMIC and all. For some of you, it will have been traumatic. It's so hard to know where to start to deal with all the thoughts and feelings that have surfaced. Sometimes it feels like you must read, listen to and watch all of the internet to find what you are looking for—not dissimilar to trying to book a holiday somewhere new: Europe or farther afield? Airbnb or hotel? Plane or ferry? The list goes on until you just capitulate and go where you went last year so you don't have to look at any more hotel reviews and risk throwing your computer out a window in a fit of uncontrollable rage and frustration.

Even I, as a psychologist, would suffer a debilitating level of overwhelm trying to establish what constitutes good stress management on the internet. I wanted to cut through all that for you. So, I read all of the internet (alright, I didn't; I just used all my clinical training and experience) and came up with what works and what is accessible. The aim of this book has always been that it is:

1. Evidence-based, i.e., I want to show you what works and what is backed by science. I don't want to waste your precious time with things that don't help.
2. Short. I want you to use it anywhere and everywhere (maybe I will even see you, a stranger, perusing it on the train! I promise I will keep my distance and not silently sidle up to you to see if you are actually reading it or have fallen asleep) so that it becomes part of your everyday life. That's where the change will happen. If I wrote something the size of *War and Peace*, you'd read it once, if that, and then use it as a doorstop.

And why should you listen to me? I'm a clinical psychologist who treats refugees with post-traumatic stress disorder (PTSD). All the people I work with are survivors of torture, war or sexual violence. It's a great job and I'm very lucky to be able to do it. But it also means I know something about stress and resilience. I have worked with refugees and clinicians across the world, from the camps of northern Iraq, training psychologists to treat PTSD in Yezidi women and girls who have been enslaved by ISIS, to helping train psychologists here in London to treat survivors and families of the Grenfell fire.

And apart from being a psychologist, I'm a human being, just like you. I laugh like you, cry like you, screw up like you. *All of the time.* And just like you, I'm climbing my own mountain of stress. I can shout out to you to avoid that big crevasse you are stumbling into and throw you a really good rope. But I fall into my own crevasses, too, and the tools and techniques you'll find in this book are the ones I use to climb out. They've transformed my life. They're the ones I tell my friends to use. And the ones I wish I'd known about when I was younger.

When I started writing this book, I had never heard of COVID-19, lockdowns, self-isolation or any of the other phrases that now trip blithely off our tongues as though we have been saying them all our lives. I had never had such a deep relationship with hand sanitizer.

I felt as we all felt—overwhelmed and afraid. This global upheaval is new to us, the curtailment of our lives jarringly different to life as we knew it. But I know from all the refugees I have worked with that the rest of the world has long suffered dislocation and trauma. Many have been lucky to avoid it for as long as we have. At the heart of the human experience is both joy and emotional pain. We cannot have one without the other. We have to make room for sadness as much as we make room for happiness.

Becoming stressilient is not about avoiding that inevitable emotional pain—it's about making room for every emotion in the face of stress. It's about turning toward, not away, from your emotions, whether you like them or not. It's about not running away from those feelings anymore. Can you imagine what it would feel like to not have to do that? How liberating would it be to focus on what matters to you instead of being in a tug-of-war with your painful emotions? What if you could put your energy into the things that would actively make your life rewarding and meaningful?

And this is where this book comes in. You picked up this book for a reason. You're intrigued by the possibility of a different way of living. Maybe the life-changing ruptures of the pandemic have asked some questions of you about how you live your life and what you want for your future. Here, you'll find the tools and techniques to help you think better, feel better and live better. You'll dig deep into what really matters to you and learn to act according to your deepest values. You'll find a way to thrive, not just survive. And I know it works, because I've taught countless people like you how to do it.

You cannot avoid life's ups and downs, and nor can I. But we can equip ourselves with the skills to navigate them in order to transform our lives. That, at least, is in our control.

So, shall we begin?

How to Use
This Book

Don't flip to the end to see what happens, it's not that kind of book. As it's small and compact, can I suggest that you read it through once before you do anything else? Then come back to the bits that help you, in whichever order works best for you.

My intention has always been that you can carry this around with you, stuffed into a handbag or tucked safely into a pocket, and turn to it when life feels overwhelming, whether you are hiding in the bathroom at a family gathering, raging in the supply closet at work or standing idly in the queue at the supermarket. I hope this book becomes dog-eared from overuse, and that you come to see it as a reliable and wise friend.

The first chapter (Brain 101) will give you a lowdown on your brain and how it works, crucial knowledge if you are going to learn to wrangle your mind a bit better. The following six chapters (How to Think Better; How to Feel Better; How to Have Perspective; How to Be Here Right Here, Right Now; How to Live Better; and How to Take Action) focus on your thinking, emotions and actions—these are the core elements of psychological flexibility. I hope by the end you can mentally touch your toes. I added How to Be Self-Compassionate and How to Understand Yourself because many years of treating patients have shown me that these are two deeply important ways of cultivating well-being.

There are many things I have not focused on here that have a positive impact on stress—sleep, diet, exercise, to name but three of the big players. My focus has instead been to concentrate on your inner world and how to navigate that more effectively so you can do the things that are important to you. Having some skills to stop your thoughts and feelings hijacking you makes it more likely that you can actually do what matters to you.

Alright, enough chat, let's get going.

Chapter 1

How to Manage Your Mind: Brain 101

"I used to think the brain was the most
important organ in the body, until I realized
who was telling me that."

—EMO PHILIPS, COMEDIAN

One of the most effective things I do in therapy is to explain how the brain works. If you are going to get the best out of your brain, then you need to know a little bit more about that thing sitting between your ears. It's the most powerful machine in the world, yet we really don't understand how to manage it. Someone needs to hand out instruction manuals at birth. Read on for the lowdown on the brain.

The Beginning

Cast your mind back. Imagine you are a cavewoman sitting outside your cave, enjoying a beautiful sunset, with a gentle smile on your face.

Now imagine being torn to shreds by the bear hiding in the trees by your cave. Because that's what happened to people who sat around chilling out. They got mauled by bears. Or lions. Or whatever roamed about looking for human snacks.

Our ancestors survived, and passed on their genes, by being super-duper hypervigilant and looking out for danger everywhere. They were a nervy bunch. But it made sense if you think about the very real threats to physical survival back then. Better to be safe than sorry and all that.

No matter that a lot of the time you didn't really see a snake in the corner of your cave, just your handbag strap (they had bags, right?), it still paid off to be very, very cautious, and so your brain evolved into a highly alert "don't get killed" machine. That's its job, and it's why your ancestors survived and why you are here. So, thanks for that, ancestors.

Now, it gets trickier. As humans began to live in groups for survival, they fared better. They were safer and more likely to survive and pass on their genes.

So now the other crucial concern our great-, great-, great-, etc., grandmothers had was to not get shunned by the group. We simply wouldn't have survived in those conditions on our own—who would kill something for us to eat if we were alone and poorly? A bit like getting someone to nip out to the store for you when you're self-isolating. Or hungover.

In Gear for Fear

Your brain is in gear for fear, and the bit of the brain most responsible for that is your amygdala. The amygdala, an unassuming little thing the size of an almond, kickstarts you into action if it thinks there's a clear and present threat. It shouts, "This is not a drill!" very loudly in your brain. It's one of the bits of your brain that evolved first, and its main interest is survival because that's the only thing that mattered. Your amygdala will put your brain and your body into high alert by initiating the fight-or-flight response. Your amygdala is important, and has helped humans to survive and evolve, but it's not the most sophisticated protagonist in your brain. It acts first and doesn't really ask any questions later.

The fight-or-flight response is evolution's way of keeping you alive. If you sense danger, then you either need to leg it or put up a fight—all your physiological responses are geared toward doing this. Your muscles tense, your heart beats faster, your breathing becomes shallow, your thoughts race . . . hang on . . . isn't that anxiety? Yes. The symptoms of anxiety are the same because, well, they're kind of the same thing. Your brain will respond in the same way to modern-day threats or stress (fears about coronavirus, work, family, status, money, health, being rejected—you name it) in a similar way to being attacked by bears. Hence being very worried about public speaking in front of your boss or overthinking a relationship crisis can trigger a fight or flight response.

The Wise Woman in Your Brain

If only you had a pal in your brain to help calm your amygdala down and manage stress . . . Well, you do! Your prefrontal cortex is like the wise woman of your brain. I like to imagine mine as Michelle Obama, but you could choose, say, Ruth Bader Ginsberg or Maya Angelou. It's situated just behind your forehead. You can give it a little stroke if you like, to show your appreciation.

The PFC is what makes us uniquely human. It's the "new" part of the brain, the part that has evolved more recently as we have started to live in more complex groups. Unlike your amygdala, this is the sophisticated part of the brain. This newer part of the brain can solve problems, plan ahead and inhibit impulses. It's the part that has helped scientists find a vaccine for COVID-19.

The PFC has access to information from your current situation and your past, so it can help you make good, effective choices in the face of stress. The problem is that it responds more slowly in the face of a threat than your amygdala, which has activated your fight-or-flight system before you can even say "prefrontal cortex." But don't panic: I will be showing you how to keep your amygdala in check so you can use your PFC buddy to better effect.

So your PFC is just super, but—of course there's a but—its ability to think about what will happen in the future (which is what problem-solving is) and to have access to past experiences means that it's also the part of us that can agonize about the past, catastrophize about the future and compare ourselves unfavorably with others.

This Modern Life

So, we've got a problem. Our old brains are still geared for fear, plus we have new brains that can worry about the future and agonize about the past. But there are no saber-toothed tigers or lions or snakes anymore. There's something worse: the modern world.

To our minds, the modern world has as many threats as it's ever had. And we respond in similar ways, which aren't always that helpful. A cavewoman looks out for life-threatening danger, and our modern minds do the same by asking, "What if I fail? Is it worth the risk?" A cavewoman doesn't use up energy unless it's crucial. Our modern minds tell us not to risk something unless we can be sure of the outcome.

A cavewoman thinks "I am not foraging in there, my friend. It went horribly wrong last time." Our modern minds say, "Who do you think you are? Once a failure, always a failure." Add in a sprinkling of comparing yourself to others on social media (because you are built to fear rejection by the group), and your mind will go into threat overdrive.

So your mind isn't trying to screw you and your life plan up; it's trying to save you from pain, because that's what it's evolved to do, but it's making a bit of a mess of it. Now that you know that your mind is well-meaning but anti-risk in any form, you can handle some of the stuff it comes out with more effectively so it doesn't hold you back. You can absolutely learn to manage your amygdala and get the best out of your PFC to respond effectively to stress.

In the following chapters I am going to teach you the skills that are crucial to being stressilient in the modern world—how to manage your thoughts and feelings so they don't hold you back, and how to live a better, more fulfilling life in the face of stress.

BOTTOM LINE

Brains have evolved to spot danger and to protect you from harm. This is great when chased by tigers, lions and bears, but less good when tackling modern day threats.

Old Brains (Don't get killed/rejected) + New Brains (What if I get rejected like last time/What if I get killed) + Modern Life (I will fail, I am a loser, I can't do this) = Tricky Minds that need managing properly with approaches based on science. Now, that's a bumper sticker I'd like.

Chapter 2

How to Think Better

"Make not your thoughts your prisons."

—WILLIAM SHAKESPEARE, *ANTHONY AND CLEOPATRA*, ACT V, SCENE II

I t all starts with your mind and the stuff that goes on in it—thoughts, memories, images. The biggest mistake I see people make is trying to change their lives without first learning how to manage their thoughts. If you don't learn to think a little better, your mind will pull you off track every time. In this chapter I will explain why the things you usually do to deal with unwanted thoughts, memories and images don't work, and what to do instead.

So, now you know that your brain is primed to look for danger and to warn you (a lot) about threats to your well-being in the modern world. You also know that your brain is very good at solving problems (even harder ones than fiendish sudoku)—it is, in fact, a problem-solving machine whose main aim is to not get killed. And that's okay, as problem-solving works very well in the external or physical world but less well in our inner worlds.

Problem-Solving Brains

Imagine a problem you have had recently—running late for a meeting, wanting to fix a leak in your roof, finding a hole in your shoe. Did your mind go to work on this problem and come up with solutions? Ring to say you will be late, call someone to fix the roof, take your shoe to the cobbler? All of them damn fine, tip-top solutions. So far, so good.

But here's the problem. We then tend to ask our problem-solving minds to also deal with the maelstrom of stuff that goes on inside us, namely thoughts, memories, images, feelings, urges and physical sensations.

I am such a loser. I am a failure. I can't do this. Had one of those lately? I am willing to bet you have. How do I know? Because nearly all of us do. Take a sneaky sideways glance at the person sitting next to you while you read this—maybe you are at work, or home or on the train, or staring out the window while we are in lockdown #86—I can guarantee you that at one time or another they have had these thoughts, too. Kerry in IT might seem like she's got her life totally sorted with her ever-positive outlook and effortless capsule wardrobe, but her mind will be giving her a beating at times, just like your mind does.

And what do you try to do with the evaluations, comparisons, judgments and reasons your mind comes up with? You try to fix or change them. You try to talk yourself out of them or you berate yourself for having them in the first place. Your mind argues both sides until you are walking around the street waving your arms while muttering darkly to yourself as other people start to cross the road. Or so I've heard.

CAGE-ing Thoughts

Attempting to change, avoid, get rid of or escape unwanted thoughts largely doesn't work, but we do it anyway
because a) we are hardwired to (see previous chapter), b) society tells us not to have negative thoughts and c) no one
shows us an alternative. I can't do much about a) and b), but
I am going to step up on c). I am going to call this attempt
to manage your thoughts CAGE:

Change
Avoid
Get rid of
Eliminate

It's not a proper psychology self-help book if I don't invent
an acronym.

I want to show you why fighting with your unwanted
thoughts doesn't work. Try something out with me. Don't
think about a white furry bear. Just don't think about that
big white bear lumbering across the frozen north. Nope,
just don't think about it. Just think about something else,
anything else but that white bear.

So? How did you get on? Thought so. White bears everywhere.

This phenomenon was investigated by Daniel Wegner, a
professor of psychology at Harvard, after coming across
this line in Dostoyevsky's account of his travels in Europe:

"Try to pose for yourself this task: not to think of a polar bear, and you will see that the cursed thing will come to mind every minute."

Wegner decided to investigate this in his lab. He found that asking people to suppress the bear actually brought it to their minds more intensely and frequently. Not only that, but trying to suppress an image of the bear meant people had to then think about the bear in order to check that they were not thinking about it in the first place.

You can see where I am going with this. The more we push unwanted thoughts out of our minds, the more they rebound on us. The more you try to push away "I am a loser," "I am ugly," "I am fat," "I am worthless," "I am a failure," the more they come back and hit you in the face. And when you try not to think about it, you have to check you aren't thinking about it, which means you are, in fact, doing the actual thing you are trying very hard not to do.

Cognitive Fusion

Getting totally tangled up in your thoughts like this is called cognitive fusion. It's like being stuck to your thoughts—think of a mouse caught in a sticky trap. The problem with being fused, or stuck, with your thoughts is that it stops you from taking action in your life, rather like the aforementioned mouse. Your thoughts, and what they say you can and cannot do, are calling the shots in your life.

When you are in a state of fusion with your thoughts, you aren't present because you are too preoccupied with trying to CAGE them. And that means you aren't present, you aren't living in line with your values and you aren't taking effective action to actually do something differently.

But It's True!

Look, we are very concerned with what is true and what isn't in the external world. And that's a good thing. Seeing a red traffic light and thinking "I won't speed through it" is a good thing. Reminding yourself you need to do your tax returns is wise. You get my drift.

The key thing to remember is that it doesn't matter whether your thoughts are true or not. I'll just let that sink in for a minute because most people find this hard to begin with, pleading, "But it *is* true!"

Where we need to let go of whether thoughts are true or not is when they are evaluations, judgments, opinions, reasons and criticisms. Let's say you think you are anxious about public speaking. That may be true. Ideally, you would take concrete steps to improve your public speaking skills if that was something that mattered to you. But too often this will happen instead:

"I'm not good at public speaking; I get too nervous. Now I have this presentation to do in front of my boss tomorrow. I know I'll blow it; I can picture myself turning red and stumbling over my words, and all my colleagues will be sniggering, especially Kerry from IT. I'm such a loser and a failure. I definitely will not get a promotion after this. I can't stand feeling like this. Maybe I'll be made redundant after the next round of cuts, which is definitely coming. What if I can't pay the mortgage? Is there enough in my savings to survive for a few months while I look for another job? I'd better research whether I can take a mortgage break. I'll have a quick look on Google even though I should prepare for tomorrow. Maybe I need to think about moving in with my parents for a bit. God, what will everyone say if I move in with my parents? They'll think I'm a loser! And they'll be right! I feel awful. I'm going to call in sick tomorrow."

Now, how did we go from thinking about delivering a presentation to moving in with the parents and sleeping in the spare room next to the unused exercise bike? Because we got fused with all the self-criticisms and judgments. Maybe in this example it's true you are a nervous public speaker. Maybe you can improve. But getting fused with it leads very quickly to a series of autopilot thoughts that propel you into a pit of despair and severely limit any useful action you could take to actually improve your presentation skills. And in the short term it works. Avoidance works. You feel better for a little bit. But it doesn't take a genius to work out that if you avoid all this stuff repeatedly, the long-term consequence is a narrowed and constricted life. And I know you don't want that, because here you are, reading this book.

There Is Another Way

But listen. I have big news. You don't have to listen to every damn thing your mind tells you about yourself and you don't have to CAGE (control, avoid, get rid of, escape) what goes on in your head either. I know, right? Crazy. This was a revelation to me. I told that friend who waved her arms around and talked to herself, too, and she also found it very helpful . . .

You can learn to manage your thoughts better not by CAGE-ing the thoughts themselves but by *changing your relationship with them*. This is crucial. You can have a thought without buying into it. Aristotle wrote, "It is the mark of an educated mind to be able to entertain a thought without accepting it." Remember that. Always good to have an Aristotle quote up your sleeve. And with practice you can do the same.

Consider your thoughts like the annoying guest at your dinner party. You didn't want to invite them but they came with your friend Brigitte from work, so now you are stuck with them. Now, you could spend all your time glaring at them, hoping they will leave (they won't), but that means you won't be attending to your other guests in the way you would like. Or you can take a different approach. You can decide you will be a good host to your unwanted guest even though you don't want to. You can be polite and flash your most charming smile, offer them a lovely cocktail and canapé (you host very sophisticated dinner parties, I must say), and continue to mingle with other guests, making sure everyone is having a delightful evening. This is a better way to spend your dinner party, rather than plotting darkly about how to lock your unwanted guest in the downstairs bathroom while neglecting your other friends who are longing for you to walk over with the mini beef wellingtons and ask them about their house renovation. The same can be said of the thoughts you don't want. Mingle gently with them, and you free yourself of having to throw them out.

Defusing Thought Bombs

So what do you do about it? Well, traditional cognitive methods where you look for evidence for and against the thought can work well. But they can get you trapped into talking yourself out of your thinking, and you won't outrun your mind, especially when it comes to judgments about yourself. It will always come up with some new way to torture you.

The answer is to create space between the thinker (you) and your thoughts. Then you can choose what to do with that thought instead of being bullied by it. I can honestly say that if you can learn to manage your thoughts effectively, you can transform your life. You, not your thoughts, will be the boss of you.

To create that space between you and your thoughts, which are exploding like bombs all over the place, you need to defuse them. Defusing thoughts means taking the power out of them, or untangling yourself from your thoughts. Remember, it's not about working out whether they are true or not.

I have collated a few of my favorite defusion exercises below. The purpose of these exercises is to help you step back and see if buying into these thoughts helps you move toward, or away from, your values in life (more of this later). Sometimes the horrid thoughts go away. Consider this a handy side effect of defusion, not the main aim, or it won't be long before you are cursing me bitterly for not getting rid of your thoughts. The question is always whether a thought helps you take action to live a rich, meaningful and vital life.

So, don your thought-bomb-disposal kit and read on.

Having Thoughts

This is one of my favorite ways to defuse from self-judgments and evaluations (Hayes et al.,1999). Try it now.

- Summon a really negative self-judgment your mind comes up with. It might be "I am a loser/ fraud/fat/worthless"—the world's your oyster.
- Spend thirty seconds to a minute really letting this judgment sink its fangs into you. Really notice how you feel as you buy into this thought.
- Now put "I am having the thought that" in front of your judgment. So it would be "I am having

the thought that I am a loser/failure/fraud," etc. If
you can write it down, even better.
- To go to ninja levels of defusion, try this sentence
  next: "I am noticing that I am having the thought
  that I am . . ."

What you should end up with is something like this:

- I am a fraud.
- I am having the thought that I am a fraud.
- I am noticing that I am having the thought that I
  am a fraud.

What do you notice? Is there a sense of distance between
you and your thoughts? Do you feel less caught up in the
thought? Now that you have that space, what does it free
you up to do differently?

Thank Your Mind

Sometimes I feel like my mind makes intrusive calls to
me, like the people who ring on your *landline* (I know,
right?) and who seem to think you have been in an accident
recently. Your mind pulls a similar trick, but you can un-
hook from it by learning to thank it for its efforts instead of
fighting with it (Harris, 2008). Also learn to give your
mind a name to supercharge your defusion exercises.

Mind: Hi, it's me. I think you should be worrying.

You: Hey, Sheila. Thanks, but I'm okay. I appreciate you are trying to help, what with your big doom-spotting antennae, but I got this.

Mind: Ha! That's not going to work. You can't brush me off so easily. If you don't have a really good worry about the impending doom in your future right now, you'll be finished by tomorrow morning.

You: Thanks for the thought, Sheila. I really do get that you are trying to help. Anything you want to add?

Mind: Ummm . . . yeah . . . just give me a second . . .

You: Look, Sheels, I got stuff to do. Laters, yeah?

Singing and Funny Voices

This is another way to reduce the power of your thoughts a bit more. Take your troublesome thought and sing it out loud (Hayes & Smith, 2005). Lots of people do it to the tune of "Happy Birthday," but I think "Mamma Mia" is a pretty good alternative—it doesn't matter what you choose. Sing it at different speeds to see what that does to the thought.

Similarly, you can say the thought in the funny voice of a character from a film, cartoon or anyone in public life. Was Mr. Bean's voice not made for this very technique? Try saying, "I am a massive failure" in Mr. Bean's voice and see what happens to your relationship with that thought.

This is in no way about mocking yourself—you are just trying to see your thoughts as just thoughts, not commandments given to you on a mountainside.

Lemons

Over a hundred years ago, a psychologist named Edward Titchener found that when words are repeated over and over again, they lose their meaning. He did it with the word "milk," but I like to do it with "lemons." Or "fork." "Fork" is such a silly word.

Try it now. Say the word "lemon" out loud forty times. I hope you aren't on the bus. What happened? I am pretty sure that the word "lemon" just became a series of meaningless sounds. And when this happens, words also begin to lose their associations and emotional valence.

Maybe "lemons" or "milk" or "fork" don't hold many problematic associations or emotions for you, but I bet the words or phrases you use to criticize yourself do—judgments like "stupid," "fat," "worthless," "bad person."

So now repeat that exercise but with your self-critical judgments. Repeat them at least forty times to take the emotional power out of them. You aren't trying to convince yourself whether your judgment is true or not. You are just trying to take the power out of the words your inner critic spews out.

What do you notice? Does the power of these words change? If it works for you, see if you can try this a couple of times during the week. Best not to do it in a meeting with your boss while you quietly chant, "Loser."

Carry Your Thoughts with You

Write your troublesome thought on a little piece of paper and put it in your purse or wallet (Hayes & Smith, 2005). The thought might be distressing or painful, but the question you need to ask yourself is whether you are willing to carry it around with you and see it for what it is—a set of words that don't dictate what you can and can't do. I have one in my wallet that reads "I am a terrible therapist." It may or may not be true, but I still go in to work every day to try to help people. When that thought comes up, I think of that piece of paper in my wallet, I acknowledge it and I move on to doing what matters to me. It's just a thought.

The Movie in Your Head

I have focused on thoughts so far, but of course a lot of us don't just think in words. We see things in vivid images (daydreams, fantasies, memories), and we can fuse with them just as we can do with thoughts.

Images have a much stronger effect on the brain than words. Seeing something vividly in your mind's eye will result in feeling emotions more powerfully than if you just think about something in words.

As with thoughts, you can get caught up with images in your head—perhaps your brain will replay a difficult encounter between you and your partner, leaving you feeling hopeless and despondent, or maybe it will create a vivid film of you losing your job, home, children and pet hamster until you are brimming over with anxiety. Essentially, your mind likes to predict doom (remember, it's trying to be your buddy and keep you safe) and then play it in your head in glorious and vivid technicolor with the title DO SOMETHING ABOUT IT NOW emblazoned across it.

And just as you push away thoughts you don't want, you've probably also pushed away images you don't want. And maybe it works in the short term—the thoughts and images go away for a bit, but as you know from our furry white bear friends, they will return with more intensity and frequency. Instead of wasting your precious mental energy on suppressing your thoughts and images, try these techniques to defuse from the films playing in your head.

And, remember, you are not trying to get rid of these images because you don't want them, you are just trying to see them for what they are.

If you are distressed by very traumatic images from the

past relating to events like abuse, violence or assault, then I strongly advise getting professional help and not trying to manage these intrusive images using the techniques below.

Television Screens

Imagine putting your troubling image on a television screen or your phone (Harris 2008). Now play around with it. Turn the image black and white, flip it upside down or make the picture fuzzy. Fast forward or rewind it double speed. The aim is not to make it go away but for you to see that this is simply an image that cannot harm you.

Turn It into a Trailer

Imagine you are at the cinema watching a trailer made up of these images. Make it one of those really cheesy ones where the voice-over is absurdly dramatic: "This time Helen will fail spectacularly and lose all she held dear. Coming soon to a mind near you."

Project It

Imagine your image anywhere and everywhere—project it onto a wall, put it on a billboard or imagine it as a piece of art in your living room.

Do I Have to Defuse from Everything? Sounds Like Hard Work . . .

You don't have to defuse from everything. In fact, fusing with thoughts can be good fun, like when you are reading a book or watching a film. You want to fuse with it and get caught up in it. And why not? As long as it doesn't stop you from living in accordance with your values (and I'm coming to that in another chapter), then knock yourself out. There wouldn't be much fun in watching Luke about to destroy the Death Star and telling yourself it's just a bunch of plastic models and there isn't really a galaxy far, far away. You want to be totally caught up in it, and to believe you really are a Jedi who can use the Force to summon the remote control from the other side of the coffee table. The problem comes when you are so fused with thinking you are a Jedi that you no longer go to work or speak to your family or friends but spend your time building life-size X-Wings out of shoeboxes and tin foil.

A good rule of thumb here is to defuse from thoughts that don't work for you and don't serve you in being the kind of person you want to be. Does buying into self-critical thoughts motivate you to work harder? Possibly in the short term, but it's usually unsustainable. Maybe you could be better at your job, or you could be a better partner or friend. But if you really want to change those things, ask yourself which approach makes you take action to actually *do* something: getting caught up in the thought "I am awful" or defusing from this thought and taking meaning-ful, values-driven action to improve your life?

A Word About Positive Thinking

At this point, most people narrow their eyes at me in a most suspicious way and say either, "What about positive thinking, then?" or, "Affirmations make me feel better. Don't take away the stuff that makes me feel better." Yes, sometimes they do. It all depends on context—when and why you use them. Sometimes it's fine to fuse with "I am super-duper brilliant at parking" or "I nailed that inter-view." But you can fuse to a point of unhealthiness—"I am such a great driver that I can drive when I am drunk," or "I am such a great surgeon I don't need to follow the rules about not harvesting organs illegally." One Donald J. Trump is a good example of fusing unhealthily with "positive" thinking.

The question is this: does fusing with your thoughts help you live the kind of life you want to live and be the sort of person you want to be? So, if positive thinking works for you, go ahead but hold it lightly. More often than not, compulsive positive thinking is a way of masking darker, difficult feelings and emotions. And guess what? No good comes of that in the long run either.

BOTTOM LINE

You can transform your life if you change your relationship to the thoughts, memories and images which go on in your head. Learning to see them just as cognitive events, not decrees from a dictator, will take their power away and create enormous freedom for you.

Chapter 3

How to Feel Better

"Our feelings are our most genuine
paths to knowledge."

—AUDRE LORDE

D o you want to feel **better** or do you want to **feel** better? The first option is about trying to feel only "positive emotions." The second one is about feeling all the emotions that show up so you can live life to the fullest, warts and all. Guess which one I am going to tell you about. Resilience is not about avoiding emotions, nor is it about being totally controlled by them: it's about becoming flexible and bending with them so you can behave in the way that matters to you. Just take a second and imagine that you can make room for any emotion that the world throws at you today—anxiety, sadness, guilt, happiness, joy, frustration, impatience—and still do the things that matter to you. Read on to find out how you can start to build enduring resilience.

Emotions: The Lowdown

Emotions are complex physiological changes that stem from your midbrain. When something happens—and this can be internal, e.g., a memory or a thought, or external, e.g., having an argument with someone or receiving bad news—the brain registers this as something it needs to pay attention to. It then prepares you to respond and take action, but this is all happening quicker than you can say, "I'm totally fine! You?"

There's a lot of debate around how many human emotions there are, but let's say there are these six basic emotions:

- Fear
- Anger
- Disgust
- Sadness
- Surprise
- Joy

Which ones do you like? Joy? Me too. Surprise might be OK, as long as it's a finding-a-diamond-down-the-back-of-the-sofa type surprise and not Jesus-there's-a-scorpion-in-my-shoe type surprise. As for the rest, well, they're a bit meh, but they are what we have evolved to feel. Again, it's no bad thing, as they have helped us survive. You know what the weirdest thing is though? We all long to feel. We seek out experiences that make us feel a certain way—we watch comedies to feel joy, horror films to feel fear and *E.T.* to feel devastated and hollow beyond measure. And who hasn't laid around listening to Joy Division to feel at one with their sadness? It's a basic human need to search out these feelings through music, art or literature, but we only like it if we can control the amount of emotion we expose ourselves to and the way in which we do it. The real problems come not with the emotions themselves, but with what we try to do to get rid of them when they appear unannounced.

Clean Pain vs. Dirty Pain

There's a lot of fake news going around about happiness. Perhaps the most pervasive story is that the normal state for humans is to be happy. Check out the list above again—not brimming with the good feels, is it? Over 30 percent of that list is given over to what we would consider "negative" emotion. We did not survive by being chilled-out and happy. Now, when we feel a so-called natural and normal negative emotion, which might be totally appropriate, we think we have to get rid of it. Imagine that you lose your job, or a relationship ends, or one of your parents becomes terminally ill—isn't it appropriate in that context to feel sad, anxious, afraid? Consider this "clean" pain, the normal emotional pain that comes for free with being a human being. The problems come when you try to CAGE (control, avoid, get rid of, eliminate) that "clean" pain by dealing with it ineffectively so you create a new kind of pain—"dirty" pain. Dirty pain is the pain you feel when you try to shut down clean pain in a way that increases your suffering— maybe you start avoiding relationships, or you drink and eat too much to make yourself feel better, or shut yourself down so much that your life becomes constricted. Ironically, the things you do to control the original clean pain start to control you and limit your life so now you have your original clean pain (e.g., sadness at the end of a relationship) plus a new dirty pain (e.g., a drinking problem), which is probably making your original emotional pain worse and taking you away from living the kind of life you want to live. Think of it this way: clean pain is inevitable if you allow yourself to care about anything in life. Dirty pain is optional if you have better ways of dealing with clean pain.

Emotions Are Actually Beach Balls

Bear with me here, but this is a really useful way of thinking about emotions (Jepsen 2014). On vacation, do you splash around in the pool trying to push a beach ball under the water? It takes a lot of energy to keep it there, right? You certainly aren't doing much else at the same time. And what happens when you let go? It bursts back up out of the water into your face with extra force, and everyone lounging by the side of the pool laughs at you while you try to pretend that you, like, totally meant to do that.

If You Want to Miss Out on Your Life, Do This

If you push away the emotions you don't like, you are a) going to get them right back in your face like a beach ball and b) going to miss out on the rest of your life because all your energy went toward trying to get rid of what you did not want to feel. We call this attempt to get rid of emotions "experiential avoidance." It is the unwillingness to stay in contact with distressing internal experiences even when doing so causes suffering in the long term.

The more I think about it, the more I believe that repeatedly pushing away unwanted emotions sits at the heart of so much unnecessary suffering. Yes, the strategies we use to avoid emotions work in the short term, so we keep doing them, but gradually they erode our quality of life and take us away from what we value.

It's not surprising that we do this. Very few of us learn how to cope with emotions in an effective way. I doubt schools teach "Openness to Emotions" after math on a Monday morning. It seems that your options are either to override the difficult emotions by swamping them with positive ones or by getting rid of them altogether.

Caging Yourself

Which of the following do you do to CAGE (control, avoid, get rid of or eliminate) your feelings?

- Drink
- Do drugs
- Eat
- Have sex

- Exercise
- Watch TV
- Surf the internet
- Criticize yourself
- Blame others
- Avoid intimacy
- Tell yourself positive affirmations

It's not an exhaustive list; feel free to add your own particular coping strategies. Of course, there's nothing wrong with those things done occasionally; I cannot stress that enough. I like stuffing my face full of chocolate biscuits in front of the TV as much as the next person. But problems arise when they become your autopilot and habitual response to your emotions, and you are using them excessively. These strategies all work in the short term (which is why we keep doing them), but if you look hard at them, the long-term consequences aren't so super—both in terms of your physical and mental health and also because those rigid coping strategies are probably taking you in the opposite direction to the things that matter deeply to you.

A History of Your Emotions

It can be helpful to ask yourself what you have learned in your life, and especially in childhood, about emotions. Think about the following:

- What emotions were off limits?
- What emotions were openly expressed?
- What did the adults around you do or say when you were upset?
- What strategies did people around you employ to deal with difficult emotions?
- Do you still use the same strategies you learned many years ago to deal with difficult emotions?

There is no such thing as the perfect "emotional" upbringing, so please don't think someone somewhere is leading a perfect life where they effortlessly sail through life's emotional punches. We all learn some helpful and unhelpful things. These questions are just a way of beginning to understand the judgments you may carry with you, and whether they still serve you.

Ask Yourself This, Not That

The key question to ask yourself is this:

"What am I willing to feel in order to live the kind of life I want?"

instead of this:

"What can I do to stop feeling this way?"

You and I are not in total control of our emotions. We can influence them at times and avoid them for a bit, but the only thing we really can control is what we actually do when our emotions show up.

Imagine that you have two dials on you. The first is an emotion distress dial. It fluctuates depending on what is happening in your life. You lose out on a promotion, your child is really ill, your dog dies—the dial will ramp itself up to ten out of ten on the distress scale. As long as there are people and things in life you care about, then there will be emotional distress in your life. Imagine that this dial is attached to you firmly between your shoulder blades. You can't reach it, so you can't adjust the dial, although you can contort yourself into all manner of peculiar positions while you try.

Now imagine the second dial is attached to your forearm. This is your willingness dial. This dial sets how willing you are to feel an emotion, whatever it is. You can reach it easily and fiddle with it. You are in total control of this dial. You now have a choice. When something, inevitably, happens that triggers an emotion you don't want, you can either turn yourself inside out trying to control the dial on your back (and even if you could reach it, you wouldn't be able to change your emotions in the long term), or you can ramp up your openness dial and accept your emotions.

What Acceptance Is Not

Before you fling this book out the window, growling that I am telling you to feel miserable for the rest of your life, just hear me out.

Acceptance of emotions is not tolerating your emotions and putting up with them while you grit your teeth. It's not sucking it up, dealing with it, enduring it, grinning and bearing it, resigning yourself to it, giving in, giving up or suppressing it. All of these things imply that you have to change your inner experiences in some way—that's not acceptance.

Accepting your emotions is about making room for what shows up even when you don't want them, like them or approve of them. Acceptance is about being willing to feel your emotions, being open to, accommodating toward, making room for, being curious about, and making space for whatever emotions are present. And why would you do that? So you can take action in line with your values. Even if you feel uncomfortable emotions, you can still do what matters to you because you aren't wasting your energy trying to CAGE your emotions.

Here's another thing acceptance is not: it's not about accepting situations like bullying or abuse or injustice. It's about making room for the emotions in these situations so that you can affect a change. Pushing down your anger and fear might keep you in a worse situation. Walking around with a rictus smile on your face saying, "It's all just great!" while you are suffering inside is incredibly painful and crushes what your pain is telling you—that this situation is not right for you. Making room for those emotions so you can do something about it might improve your life, and the lives of others, significantly. What would have happened if Nelson Mandela, Rosa Parks or Emmeline Pankhurst had never listened to their emotional pain?

Wise Guides

Instead of thinking of your emotions as irksome things to be controlled, consider them wise guides who have something to teach you about what matters to you deep in your heart. There's a certain amount of wisdom in your painful feelings. They tell you what matters to you. You don't feel sad, angry, afraid or upset about things you don't give a damn about.

Imagine that I am a very clever wizard-y type, top of my class at Hogwarts, and I could do an amazing spell that means you feel no sadness, fear, anxiety, frustration, impatience or anything else you don't like (eat your heart out, Hermione Granger). But the flip side of this spell is that you can't feel joy, happiness, love, contentment, pleasure or any of the stuff you do like. What would you choose? Most people tell me that, if that's the choice, they don't want my weird spells. Most people don't want a life devoid of all feeling. What most of us do need, however, are better ways to manage those feelings so they don't get in the way of us living the life we want.

Don't Fight, Navigate

Instead of fighting with your emotions, learn to sail through them. Here's an exercise to practice making room for feelings so you can learn to navigate them rather than struggle with them. Try to do a little bit each day, and remember you don't have to accept every feeling 24/7. We all need a bit of distraction and avoidance sometimes but do try to make room for some of the feelings you always try to avoid.

Defuse

The idea that we can learn from painful emotions is not one we sit easily with, and perhaps you are gnashing your teeth a little as you read this. But this is where your defusion skills from the previous chapter come into play. Notice that your mind is saying, "No way am I doing that, crazy lady," and thank it for its efforts so you can keep taking action and do this exercise. Remember that sneaky thoughts might show up, like, "Why am I having this feeling?" or, "What's wrong with me?" or, "Why do I feel like this?" Again, use your defusion skills to step away from your mind and continue.

Notice

Emotions are felt in the body, and noticing them is the first step. So let's do a quick scan so you notice where you are feeling whatever you are feeling. This should take a couple of minutes, but you can make it longer if you want. The aim is not to relax but to ascertain what you are feeling in your body.

- Close your eyes and take a few deep breaths.
- Notice where your body touches the chair or your feet touch the floor.
- Notice the sensation of breathing in and out.
- Notice the air entering your body and chest, and notice the way your chest rises and falls as you breathe.
- Now see if you can notice a feeling you usually avoid—perhaps sadness, guilt, fear or anxiety. If nothing comes to you, think of a time recently when you felt an unwanted emotion. Try to make that memory vivid so that you feel those emotions you did at the time.
- Scan through your body, working down from your head to your neck, shoulders, chest, stomach, arms, legs and feet to see what physical sensations you feel and have an urge to get rid of.

Label

What is that you are feeling? Say to yourself, "I am noticing a feeling of anxiety/frustration/irritation"—complete as appropriate.

This seems easy, but actually we rarely take the time to notice what we feel and to name it. Learning to label what you feel is a powerful experience if you are not in the habit of doing it. Try to see if you can learn how you feel inside your body when a certain emotion is present and how it differs from other emotions. What does sadness feel like for you? How is it different from boredom or frustration? Start to learn what your emotions feel like.

Explore

Time for role play, but not in a weird, creepy way. Imagine you are a scientist investigating this sensation in the body (I like to imagine myself as one of those formidable Edwardian ladies who wore big hats and collect things in nets) and you've never seen anything like this before. Ask yourself:

- Where in my body do I feel this?
- If I draw an outline around it, what shape would it be?
- What color is it?
- What texture is it?
- Does it have a temperature—hot or cold?
- Does it feel near the surface or deep inside?
- Is it moving or still?

Try to notice any other physical qualities it may have as you notice it.

Breathe

As you notice all the features of this emotion, just see if you can breathe around this feeling and make space for it to be there. Imagine that you can expand around this feeling and make room for it. You don't need to do anything else, just see if you can sit with it.

Be the Sky

Imagery can be your ally in this practice. Imagine that you are the sky, and the weather represents your emotions (Harris 2009). The weather is sometimes nice, sometimes nasty. It is ever-changing, yet the sky can always make room for it. And just as the weather can never harm the sky, no matter how fierce the storm, so your emotions cannot harm you. Are they uncomfortable? Yes. Unwanted? Yes. Unasked for? Yes. Harmful in themselves? No.

Hold It Gently

Starting to make room for emotions after a lifetime of doing pretty much the opposite is a big ask and can be a very powerful experience, so be kind to yourself as you do this. Difficult memories and thoughts will arise, and that's normal and to be expected. See if you can touch what these painful experiences are telling you about what is important to you. Imagine that you can hold your emotions gently, like a delicate butterfly or a crying child.

Feelings May Change. They May Not.

As with defusing from thoughts, a pleasant side effect of accepting emotions is that the unpleasant experiences may go. While you will of course welcome this, don't expect it every time or make it your aim, otherwise you are back to taking a non-accepting stance with your emotions. It's fine if they change and it's fine if they don't.

Urge Surfing

Emotions sometimes lead us to feel urges to do something about them, and more often than not it's about trying to change the experience and situation we are in. Quite often we give in to the urge to eat the family-size bar of chocolate, have the third martini, shout at someone who is annoying us or surf the internet looking at panda cubs (er, I hear this happens) instead of doing the other things that are important to us. The consequence is that when we give in to the urge, the feeling we don't want goes away so we learn to keep doing it.

Of course, if none of these behaviors get in the way of valued living in the long term, then stuff your face, drink your fill and stay glued to the Panda-Cam. But I suspect if you are doing this excessively, and yielding to every urge, then something isn't going that well for you.

We give in to urges because we feel that, if we don't, the urge will tsunami itself over us and we won't be able to cope. And because we then do something to get rid of it, we never find out that there is no tsunami and that the waves of your urge will just ebb and flow, breaking on the shore and minding their own business.

The alternative strategy to resisting or controlling urges is to learn to urge surf. Urge surfing is a term coined in the 1980s by two American psychologists working with addiction (Marlatt & Gordon 1985), so they knew a thing or two about unhelpful urges. Instead of trying to resist or fight our urges, they suggested that we can learn to surf them and see that they naturally ebb and flow, just as waves in the sea do. Sounds nice, no?

Urge surfing uses all the techniques you have used above. Here's how to do it:

- Notice the urge in your body. Where do you feel it?
- Notice, too, what your mind is doing. Is it egging you on to give in to the urge, or telling you that you can't handle it, or conjuring pictures of how good you will feel if you succumb? Defuse from these thoughts and images using the techniques in the previous chapter.
- Label it—say "I am having the urge to . . ."

- Now just breathe into the urge and let it be there. Don't try to fiddle with it.
- Notice how the urge ebbs and flows. The urge may increase or decrease.
- Notice how you have a space between the experience of the urge and the action you take.
- You now have a choice as to how you respond. Ask yourself what action you can take that will be in line with your values.

Remember Your Why

By making room for these unpleasant, difficult and unwanted inner experiences, you are working toward living in accordance with your values. You aren't exposing yourself to emotions just for kicks—there are better ways to get thrills. One of the great gifts accepting emotions gives you is telling you what is really important to you in life. Your defusion and acceptance skills will be crucial when we come to helping you find out what you care deeply about in life.

BOTTOM LINE

It's ok to feel whatever you feel. No emotion is off-limits, no matter what your mind tells you. Learning to make room for whatever feelings and sensations in your body come your way allows you to ditch unhelpful coping strategies in favor of behaviors which help you be the kind of person you want to be and live the kind of life you want to live. Not only that, but by making room for your feelings, you choose wisdom and knowledge. And with knowledge comes the power to take transformative action.

Chapter 4

How to Have Perspective

"Know Yourself"

—INSCRIPTION FROM THE TEMPLE
OF APOLLO AT DELPHI

K nowing yourself is more than the sum of your thoughts and feelings about yourself and the world around you. If you want to take a truly bigger-picture perspective and develop deeper self-awareness to really "know yourself," then you are going to have to tap into something else. I'll be going into some deep ideas here, so put on your black turtleneck, get an espresso and light up a metaphorical Gauloise.

Leaves On A Stream

First, try out this exercise with me (Hayes & Smith 2005) and then let's chat.

- Find a comfortable position and close your eyes or keep them fixed on a spot.
- Imagine that you are sitting at the edge of a gently flowing stream. There are leaves floating past on the stream. Feel free to imagine this scene however you wish.
- Over the next couple of minutes, take every thought that pops into your head and put it on a leaf and let it float by.

- It doesn't matter if the thoughts are negative or positive, terrible or wonderful, just pop them on a leaf and let them float by.
- Notice that there's a part of you creating these thoughts and putting them on the leaves and also making judgments about this exercise and how you are doing it.
- Now notice that there's another part of you that is noticing the part of you doing all the thinking.
- It is normal and natural that your attention will wander. As soon as you realize this is happening, just acknowledge it and come back to the exercise.
- And notice that there's part of you that can notice when you get distracted, and that can bring your attention back.
- Again and again, you will get distracted, that's normal. Just notice how your thoughts come and go constantly, but that part of you that notices those thoughts is always there.

Wow, a lot of noticing. So let's unpack it a bit. I am sure that a lot of stuff popped up in your mind—thoughts about yourself, the exercise, what you need to do today. That was your "thinking self" at work. But did you also notice that you could *notice* your thinking self at work? That is so meta it makes my head hurt, and I haven't even really started yet. The part of you that does the noticing is something we don't really have an everyday word for, but let's call it your observing self. And I think you are going to like it.

Your Thinking Self

Your thinking self is made up of all your thoughts, images, memories, feelings, physical sensations you have or experience about yourself, other people and the world at large. As you know from earlier chapters, being able to think about things is important, but getting too tangled up in all that mind-y stuff isn't always helpful. The thinking self is like the ticker at the bottom of the screen you see on twenty-four-hour news channels where everything seems to be classified as "BREAKING NEWS!" It's much the same in our minds, but with a constant stream of thoughts and images. You probably spend a lot of time interacting with the world from your thinking self perspective, and more often than not, being very caught up in what it tells you.

Your Observing Self

Here's the deep bit. Whenever you think, judge, evaluate, recall, imagine, or reason with something, there's a separate part of you that is noticing everything your mind does. It can notice you noticing your thoughts, or notice you watching, or notice you hearing—just as it did in the exercise at the start of this chapter. Or it can notice you reading this right now. It's there right now as you read this. Perhaps you are reading this and thinking, "Loving this little book" or "What a total waste of money, I could have spent It on chips." As you do that, your observing self is there noticing you reading and thinking.

Or perhaps you find as you read this, you are getting distracted. Perhaps you are thinking about doing laundry or wondering whether you need more canned tomatoes (the answer to that is always yes). And when you noticed that you were distracted and brought your attention back to reading this (I hope that's what you did, or maybe you've gone to sort your colors from your whites), it was your observing self who did that.

Being able to access this part of yourself is key to developing deeper self-awareness and perspective that goes beyond what your thinking self creates. You will be able to take the ultimate "big picture" perspective. Next time Zoe in Marketing asks you to do a "blue sky thinking" exercise and you feel like jamming your pen in your eye, ask her instead if you can all tap into your observing selves—that's taking a real big-picture perspective. Then you can notice your thoughts and judgments when she says "no" through gritted teeth. You can even notice her noticing you for extra observing self points. But I'd stop there before you get fired.

When I first learned about this "other" part of myself, I felt I had a stalker in my head peering at me in a slightly creepy way through the windows of my mind, or something a bit like the Eye of Sauron watching me as I struggled through the Mordor of life. But, once you get used to the idea, you'll see how being an observer of your internal world can be an immensely powerful perspective-taking tool.

Who Even Are You?

If I ask you to tell me about yourself, I imagine your response to this will be a series of "I am" statements. "I am a parent. I am a brain surgeon. I am a sibling. I am tidy. I am tardy. I am kind. I am overweight. I am healthy. I am shy." And so on.

It is important to have these stories about ourselves or labels for the roles we play because it gives us some sense of coherence. The problems arise when we have a white-knuckle grip on those labels. We may not always play the roles we have now. How will we cope with that if we have defined ourselves solely by those roles? How will we live meaningful lives in accordance with our values if we rigidly hold onto the labels we give ourselves, whether they are negative or positive?

Sure, you can defuse from thoughts and accept feelings, just as I have shown you. But being able to interact with the world from your observing self can be a much more powerful way to access a stable sense of self from where you can cope more effectively with life's challenges.

As you might recall, from chapter 3 (How to Feel Better), your thoughts and feelings are like the weather, but you, my friend, are like the sky, which cannot be harmed by any experience. The sky is your observing self—it is stable, ever present and unchanging. Many people who have been through traumatic experiences talk about connecting with this part of themselves. Even though they have been hurt physically and emotionally, there is a part of them that cannot be harmed by their experience.

Be the Board

To help further your understanding of the thinking and the observing self, consider this Chessboard Metaphor (Hayes et al. 1999).

Imagine that you are taking part in a game of chess, perhaps at one of those nice outdoor tables in parks where charming elderly folk spend their afternoons. Your negative thoughts and feelings are the black pieces, the more positive thoughts and feelings are the white pieces. Every time a negative thought or feeling pops up like "I am a failure/anxious/unsuccessful," you try to outmaneuver it by playing a white piece like, "That's not true, I am actually a good sort." And for a moment, all is well. But the problem is that as soon as you play a white "positive" piece, your mind will play another black "negative" piece because, well, that's what minds do. And so you go on fighting the black pieces with your white pieces, fighting the negative with the positive. The bigger problem is that the game never ends—there are an infinite number of pieces, and the board stretches on forever in all directions. This is not what you intended—you only wanted a nice game of chess and a little walk around a park, and now you are here forever trapped in an exhausting and futile battle with your own internal world with little prospect of stopping for lunch.

Instead of trying to outflank your negative thoughts like a grand master, consider yourself not the player of the game but the very board itself. You can let thoughts and feelings be present and run through you, but you don't need to get caught up in this battle. You are the board—stable and strong. You are both able to contain and observe the match. And when you are the board you are free to do other, more meaningful things with your life while your pieces do their thing.

Befriending Your Observing Self

Here's a good way to start rolling with your observing self. In this exercise (*The Continuous You* by Harris 2009), X can be your thoughts, feelings, emotions, physical sensations, urges, your physical body and all the roles you have in your life. Try this out a couple of times a day.

1. Notice X.
2. There is X and there you are noticing X.
3. If you can notice X, you cannot be X.
4. X is always in flux; it changes constantly. The part of you that notices X does not change.

The key points here are that your internal world is constantly changing, but the part that notices all of that never changes, and that if you can notice all of that *then you cannot be it*—you are separate from it.

The Continuous You

This exercise (Sinclair & Beadman 2016) comes in three parts, an excellent trilogy. Stick with it—it can be a very powerful experience. Read through it all first, and then have a go.

Part 1:

- Start by closing your eyes and bringing your attention to your breath. Notice the feeling of your breath entering your body through your nostrils, and follow your breath down to your lungs and out again. Breathe in this way for a couple of minutes.
- When you are ready, bring a painful memory (not a deeply traumatic one) to mind from your childhood. Perhaps it might be a time you felt rejected by a friend, or a time you felt isolated. Start to notice what you can see and hear in this memory as your younger self. What is going through your mind—what thoughts or worries

are present? What do you feel in your body?
What emotions are present?
- If you can notice all these thoughts, senses and
emotions, you cannot be them.
- Those thoughts, sights, sounds, emotions,
physical sensations all change and fluctuate, but
the YOU who is noticing them does not change.
It has always been the same, and it has always
been there.
- Notice now that there is somebody behind the
eyes of this younger self. See if you can experience
being this observer. What would you say to your
younger self about their struggles and their
suffering?

Part 2:

- Now bring to mind another painful memory
from your more recent past. As you did with
your younger self, notice what is going through
your mind. What emotions do you feel? Where
in your body do you feel them? What do you see
and hear?
- If you can notice all these thoughts, senses and
emotions, you cannot be them.
- Those thoughts, sights, sounds, emotions,
physical sensations all change and fluctuate, but

the YOU who is noticing them does not change.
It has always been the same, and it has always
been there.

- Notice now that there is somebody behind the
  eyes of this recent self. See if you can experience
  being this observer. What would you say to your
  recent self about their struggles and their
  suffering?

Part 3:

- Now start to notice what is going through your
  mind at this very moment. Notice what emotions
  you feel and where you feel them in your body.
  What do you see and hear in this moment?
- If you can notice all these thoughts, senses and
  emotions, you cannot be those thoughts, senses
  and emotions.
- These thoughts, sights, sounds, emotions,
  physical sensations all change and fluctuate, but
  the YOU who is noticing them now is not
  changing. It has always been the same, it has
  always been present and it always will.
- Notice now that there is somebody behind your
  eyes noticing these experiences at this very
  second. See if you can experience being this
  observer. This observer was with your younger

self, your recent self and will be with your future
self.

- What message would you like to send yourself
about any pain or suffering you are struggling
with right now?

What was that like? Strange? Powerful? Unsettling? I, like
many others, certainly found it to be all those things when
I first practiced this, but it has now become an important
part of how I relate to myself. There is also, I think, a comfort in this deep, stable sense of self, which has always been,
and always will be, with you.

Told you it was deep.

BOTTOM LINE

It is by accessing a profound sense of "you" that you can
really begin to know yourself beyond the labels you give
yourself. You can find space away from that mind-generated
content and choose to do what matters to you. When you
can access a part of you that is truly safe and stable, you have
an immensely powerful resource at your disposal.

Chapter 5

How to Be Right Here, Right Now

"The ability to be in the present moment is a major component of mental wellness."

—ABRAHAM MASLOW, PSYCHOLOGIST

H ands up if your mind wanders. Everyone? Yes, even you in the back. We all have minds that are like restless, fidgety toddlers who can't sit still. We are pitched between rehashing the past and catastrophizing about the future. Rarely are we in the present moment, which is where all the action happens. Developing skills to help you stay in contact with the present moment will enable you to harness deeper levels of awareness so that you can live more effectively.

Where's Your Head At?

Human beings do not like to be in the present moment. A Harvard study (Killingsworth & Gilbert 2010) found that people spend 47 percent of their time thinking about things that aren't happening now, have already happened or may or may not happen. The authors of the study found that mind-wandering is an excellent predictor of people's happiness, writing that "how often our minds leave the present and where they tend to go is a better predictor of our happiness than the activities in which we are engaged." You can be doing the best activity in the world—watching zebras at a remote watering hole on safari, dunking biscuits in your tea, winning an Oscar—but if you cannot be present you will not appreciate it. Sounds about right. We are a very "non-present" bunch, pinged from past to future like the hapless ball in a game of pinball, leaving us with the feeling that life is out of control and that we are at the mercy of random thoughts and emotions. You may recall that your mind's ability to time travel better than Doctor Who is a uniquely human thing, as is its ability to compare, evaluate and judge. Other animals don't spend their time worrying about whether the burrow next door is worth more, especially following this latest slump in the burrow market, and was the extension really worth it? And who has just moved into that nest down the road? Our ability to do this repeatedly can lead to immense dissatisfaction with life.

Rumination

Rumination or cud-chewing is the process by which a cow regurgitates previously consumed feed and chews it further. Lovely. Cows spend more time chewing during rumination than they do when they eat. Excessive dwelling in the past, going over and over the same events, is a psychological kind of rumination. We literally chew over and vomit up old events, hurts, injustices over and over again. Doing this to some degree is, of course, natural. We seek to understand what happened and to manage the distress it causes. If a good friend treats you unkindly, you would think about that for a while. If someone in the office uses your favorite mug, when they know that you have strict rules about that sort of thing, you would rightly chew over this injustice. But done repeatedly and excessively, it is an ineffective way of dealing with distress and serves only to make you feel more psychologically and physiologically stressed by taking you out of contact with the present moment.

Worrying

If you aren't ruminating about the past, you are probably worrying and catastrophizing about the future. Again, it's a human superpower to think about the future and plan for it. A bit of worry is a good thing. If worrying that you might get cancer means that you are diligent about being screened, then super. That's useful worrying. But if you are so worried about it that you won't even go to a doctor, then that's not serving you well. Worrying is a sneaky and crafty character, often masquerading as problem-solving and planning. It sidles up to you, promises to make life a bit easier. As with alcohol, you must worry responsibly and in moderation.

Autopilot

When your mind wanders, it switches into autopilot mode. Having an autopilot mode can be very helpful in allowing you to do things quickly and effectively without too much conscious thought or effort. Getting up in the morning, having a shower and making coffee do not need to be the subject of deep daily reflections and awareness. You'd never leave the house, which, while seductive and tempting at times, is not generally a good thing for the old mental wellness. The problem arises when we live too much of life on autopilot, which leads to mindlessness. Examples of mindlessness include:

- Not being able to remember what you've just read (is this happening to you right now?!)
- Watching TV while on your phone and scrolling aimlessly through the news, Facebook, Twitter and Instagram
- Not noticing different flavors or textures in food, so you just shovel it in without paying attention
- Not paying attention to someone who is telling you something important
- Not being able to acknowledge and be open to unwanted thoughts and feelings

Letting your mind function on autopilot all the time is not going to enable you to live a more satisfying life. If you want to live in a more deliberate way, then you need to deactivate your autopilot a bit more often and take control.

Contacting the Present Moment

Both worrying and rumination, in cahoots with our time-traveling minds and our propensity for autopilot and mindlessness, take us out of contact with the present moment. And that's too bad, as this is where the magic happens. The actions you can take to change your life happen here and now, not in the past and not in the future. Having a moment-to-moment awareness of what is happening in your mind, body and the world around you allows you to appreciate the fullness of each moment, whether it is something you view as negative or positive.

Mindfulness

I bet you were wondering how long it would take before I mentioned mindfulness. And with good reason—you can't move for mindfulness these days. It's no bad thing—mindfulness has strong empirical evidence for reducing stress. The problem is that there are a lot of mindfulness myths and misconceptions out there. So let's start with a little mindfulness tutorial.

What Is It?

Jon Kabat-Zinn, who is widely credited with bringing mindfulness to a Western audience, defines mindfulness as "the awareness that arises through paying attention, on purpose, in the present moment, nonjudgmentally."

Well. This isn't so easy for your mind, which cites its chief hobbies as not paying attention on purpose, not being present and judging everything in sight. The good, yet possibly predictable, news is that repeated practice of mindfulness can yield big stress reduction results.

What It Isn't

Mindfulness is often practiced in ways that are far removed from what it is really about. Mindfulness is not relaxation, distraction, positive thinking or a way to police your thoughts. Relaxation does happen sometimes when you practice mindfulness, but consider it a nice bonus, not the aim. The aim is simply to notice your internal and external world with an attitude of curiosity, openness and non-judgment so that you can live more effectively. If it sounds a lot like the skills of defusion, acceptance and perspective-taking that I've told you about, then top marks for paying attention because mindfulness is implicit in all of those processes.

So how do you contact this elusive present moment? You develop and practice skills based on mindfulness. Here are a few to get you started.

Mindfulness of the Breath

This is by far the simplest way to get started with some mindfulness.

- Sit with your feet on the floor, your back straight and either close your eyes or focus on a particular spot.

- Let your mind come to your breath.
- Notice the sensations of breathing with curiosity. Notice the feeling of air entering through your nostrils and going down into your lungs. Notice the feeling of exhaling, how your chest and shoulders might rise and fall.
- Your mind will wander as you do this, but start to notice when this happens and just bring your attention back to your breath.

Do this for a few minutes every day. That's all you need to start with. Remember, it's not about avoidance, distraction or relaxation. You are just noticing. The ability to keep bringing your wandering mind to the present will strengthen your focusing and attention skills.

Dropping an Anchor

This is a great exercise to do when you find yourself in an emotional storm (Harris 2009). It will keep you steady so you can choose what actions you take rather than switching on your autopilot.

- Push your feet hard into the floor.
- Sit forward in your chair, and straighten your back.
- Press your fingertips together, move your elbows, move your shoulders. Feel your arms

moving, all the way from your fingers to
shoulder blades.
- Notice that there's a lot of pain here, that you're
  struggling. Notice there's also a body around that
  pain—a body that you can move and control.
  Just notice your whole body now—hands, feet,
  back.
- Now look around the room and notice five things
  you can see.
- And also notice three or four things you can hear.
- So notice there's something very painful here that
  you're struggling with.
- And notice your body, which you can control, in
  the chair.
- Notice that there's you here with these feelings.

In a very challenging emotional storm, you might like to
cycle through this exercise a few times until you feel more
in the present moment. Remember, the aim of this is not
to make anything go away, even if it feels unpleasant, but
to be present with whatever you feel and take a different
action. If, for example, you find yourself regularly CAGE-
ing (controlling, avoiding, getting rid of, escaping) difficult and unwanted thoughts and feelings, this is a good
way to both start noticing them and making room for
them.

Mindfulness of This Very Book

Well, as you are here, with this book, you might as well take a good, mindful turn with it. Talk about value for money.

- Notice the weight of the book in your hand.
- Notice the urge you have to read on, so captivated are you. Or notice the urge you have to toss it into the nearest garbage can.
- Look at the book with curiosity, and notice its color, texture and, if you are alone, its smell. If you are in public, I leave it to your discretion as to whether sniffing books is a socially acceptable act.
- Notice what your mind is saying about this book or the exercise itself. Acknowledge those thoughts, but just let them ebb and flow, and bring your attention back to the book.
- Try to do this for a couple of minutes—observing with curiosity and noticing your thoughts as you do so. When your mind wanders, which it will, just bring your attention back.

Mindfulness of Music

This is a very good way to learn to flexibly switch your focus and attention (Hayes 2019).

- Put on a piece of music you like, as long as it has multiple instruments.

- Set a timer at one-minute intervals.
- To begin with, focus on all the instruments but then turn your attention to just one instrument.
- After a minute, turn your attention to another instrument.
- End by turning your attention to all the instruments.
- Repeat two or three times.

54321

I find this exercise helps me focus when, for example, I am trying to write a book and my mind wanders, and I fuse with making up excuses to publishers and agents as to why I have produced nothing for the last year. This allows me to ground myself in the present moment and return to my task more quickly rather than falling down the rabbit hole of rumination. It looks something like this:

- Sit down to do a task.
- Get distracted by thinking about the past or future.
- Occasionally enjoy this process, but 99 percent of the time feel worse as mind wanders to many and varied doom-laden scenarios frequently culminating in failure/destitution/rejection/death.
- Notice this mind-wandering is happening and that it clearly does not serve completion of the task.

- Take mindful action and contact the present moment.
- Breathe deeply.
- Look around.
- Name five things you can see.
- Name four things you can hear.
- Name three things you can touch.
- Name two things you can smell.
- Name one thing you can taste.
- Refocus and return to the task.

Of course, there are days when your mind roves more than others and you will have to repeat this task, but with increased practice, focus will return more quickly.

Mindful Listening

If you want to deepen your relationships with others, then take a little time to start developing your mindful listening skills. If you have ever felt that someone is really listening to you, then you will understand how powerful it can be. You have to be fully present to be aware of what is being said and to connect with that. This means not only detaching from your phone as someone talks, but really bringing your attention to what they are saying. I am not suggesting that you do this all the time, as normal conversation has a lot of back-and-forth banter, but sometimes it pays to be really present. Here are some tips:

- Be genuinely curious. Don't assume you know what someone will say and preempt them.
- Be aware of your internal dialogue but keep present. Your intention might be to be present, but your mind will have other ideas, offering up a series of thoughts, comments and judgments. Chipping in with "That was like when I . . ." or "I know how that feels because . . ." takes you away from really attending to what someone is saying. Be aware of your thoughts, but see if you can treat them like an annoying song on the radio in the background. They're there, but your attention can be here.
- Reflect back. OK, this feels weird but does really help someone to feel heard. Summarize what you have heard them say, but in your own words, or say, "So, what I heard you say was . . ."
- Ask for clarity. You are coming to this conversation with a mindful stance, so let go of judgments and assumptions. I often ask my clients, "Can I check I have understood that correctly?"
- Ask questions but don't interrupt. In therapy, I will say, "Can I ask a question?" and clarify feelings, thoughts, physical sensations, not just facts. I am not here to take a deposition but to understand someone's experience on a deeper level.

If you think this will feel very weird, then you are right. It does. But you won't be doing it all the time—your friends will freak out and edge politely away from your newfound and intense listening skills. But when someone you care about is suffering, or needs you to really listen, then this is something to try.

BOTTOM LINE

Regular mindfulness practice will help you reduce stress and improve your focus and flexibility, and who doesn't want that? Think of it as an attitude to cultivate—like being cool and wearing sunglasses all day even when it's cloudy—rather than something you "do" every now and then. Remember, it's a way of contacting the present moment so you can live with more purpose, not a way of getting rid of irksome stuff. Leo Tolstoy once wrote, "If, then, I were asked for the most important advice I could give . . . I should simply say: in the name of God, stop a moment, cease your work, look around you." Wise words. But not as wise as the incomparable Ferris Bueller: "Life moves pretty fast. If you don't stop and look around once in a while, you could miss it." Word, Ferris, word.

Chapter 6

How to Live Better

"Everything can be taken from a man but one
thing: the last of the human freedoms—to
choose one's attitude in any given set of
circumstances, to choose one's own way."

—VIKTOR E. FRANKL, PSYCHIATRIST AND
AUSCHWITZ SURVIVOR

So now we come to the crux of it all—why are you here? I am guessing you picked up this book because you want to know how to live a bit better, how to negotiate the ever-present stresses of life in a different way. Maybe you want to thrive—not just survive—and to find that elusive "why." Too often we live each day on autopilot going through the motions. Head down, collar up and plowing on. When we do look up it's usually to compare our lot with other people's and to think about how we can get more stuff to make us feel better. Those things often work in the short term, which is why we keep doing them, but in the long term it leads to a sense that life lacks purpose and meaning. To live a richer, more meaningful, authentic and vital life, you need to get in touch with something that you have either never thought or been asked about or have lost touch with—your values.

Values

Values are the secret weapon of well-being. They are what will motivate, inspire and guide you to thrive in the good times and negotiate the bad times. Values, in short, are the life directions you choose and what you can use to guide you through life. Think of them as an internal compass helping you point yourself in the right direction. Values are how you choose to treat yourself and other people. They are reflections of what you truly care about, deep down in your heart. When was the last time you really took time to think about what really matters to you? To stop for a moment and ask yourself, "What do I want to stand for in this life?" Probably not very recently. We don't ask ourselves or others this question, yet it can have a significant and powerful impact.

Studies looking at values (Cohen & Sherman 2014; Jordt 2017) have found that simply focusing on values helped protect minority students from internalizing the harmful cultural presumption that they could not perform as well academically as their better-off peers.

The intervention was extremely straightforward. African American and Latino students were asked to identify what they valued in life and to write about it for ten to fifteen minutes. They wrote about a wide range of values, including family, friendships, music, politics, creativity, dance and religion. That's it. *C'est tout.* Nothing fancier required than a bit of thought and a pen and paper. And what did the researchers find from this simple intervention? They found that these students went on to close the gap in their academic achievement between themselves and their fellow white students. Not bad for a few minutes spent just focusing on what really mattered to them before Monday morning's Biology class.

Laboratory studies also show how having a "why" for doing something can have a powerful effect. In a study by Smith et al. (2018) participants were first asked to perform a cold presser task. A cold presser task involves immersing a hand in freezing cold water for a bit—in this case a maximum of five minutes. Participants were then allocated to either a values condition, where they spent thirty minutes focusing on their values in relation to the cold presser task, or to the control condition, where they watched a slideshow about the wonders of the world. They were then asked to perform the cold presser task again. The researchers found that those who had focused on their values were now more able to tolerate acute pain and distress despite both groups finding the distress equally bad. In other words, the values intervention did not make the subjective ratings of pain and distress any less, but it did alter participants' response to that distress. In short, the fact they had a "why" (because they had identified their values) to tolerate pain made all the difference. Now, let's be clear. I am not suggesting you plunge your hands into the nearest icy puddle, turn your face to the sky and await revelation. Sticking your hands in icy water is presumably of not much use to you unless you are a member of the coast guard or you like doing the dishes in very cold water. I am, however, asking you to think about what would be open to you if you had a "why." What would you be able to accept—anxiety, fear, risk of rejection—in the service of acting on your values? If you have values, you have a why, and if you

have a why, then you have a reason to open up to the uncomfortable feelings that come with pursuing a meaningful
and vital life.

What Values Are

Before you and I skip off together, let's be clear about
what values are and what they aren't. It will make life easier
down the road.

Values Are Freely Chosen

Values are about what matters to you, not what you
think other people want you to value. Women are often
very good at putting the values of others first at the ex-
pense of their own. We may be using values to guide us
that aren't our own but are expected of us. This can lead
to feeling that you are inauthentic in how you live your
life or a sense that you are lacking in purpose. Maybe, for
example, you have always been told you are conscientious
and diligent although actually you'd much rather be a
spontaneous, fly-by-the-seat-of-your-pants kinda gal but
you've never dared express that part of yourself lest you
disappoint others. One way to think about this is to ask
yourself about your secret values. What would you value
if no one knew and you never, ever had to tell anyone
about it?

Values Are Self-Reinforcing

Values are also not about how other people respond. You may choose to be guided by kindness, but others may not always show you that back. What do you do then? If you were only ever kind to get kindness back, well, then arguably that isn't a value you really hold dear. The outcome of acting on values is never assured, which is an uncomfortable thing to get your head around. Values have an intrinsic reward in themselves and need to be self-reinforcing, for you cannot truly control other people's responses, however hard you try, but you can control your own behavior in what you say or do.

At this point you may start to feel a bit antsy, and I wouldn't blame you. But hear me out—I am not saying that if you have someone in your life who is cruel and unkind to you, that you should persevere in being kind to them. Not at all. At that point you mindfully reevaluate whether having this person in your life fits with your values about how you want to be treated. I am guessing it doesn't. The point I am making is that you choose values because they matter to you, not because they get you results from other people or free cappuccinos because you are nice to the lady in the coffee shop. Be kind to her because you value kindness, not because you could get a decaf, semi-skinny vanilla-hazelnut mocha chocaccino or whatever.

Values Are Ongoing Qualities of Action

Consider values as verbs; they are the way in which you do something, not something you achieve. Getting married or moving in with someone, for example, is a goal. Once you've done it, you've done it. Check it off the list. But how do you want to conduct yourself as a partner in that relationship? If you value being loving, for example, does that all stop the second you get married and achieve that goal? You don't achieve being "loving"—you bring that quality in your behavior with the other person even when you don't feel like it. And let's face it, quite often that's what relationships are all about, whether they are with your spouse, parents, children, colleagues or pets.

Values Are Powerful

Nowhere has the power of values been more movingly and strikingly articulated than in Viktor Frankl's autobiography of his time in Auschwitz. Frankl was a Jewish psychiatrist who was imprisoned in the notorious concentration camp during the Second World War. He survived and wrote a memoir of the horrendous things he both saw and experienced. What is so valuable about his account is his observation about what kept people going in the most extreme circumstances. It was not, he wrote, the strongest who survived. It was those who had a "why"—those who had a reason to live and who chose their own response even in the worst and darkest of circumstances:

> *"We who lived in concentration camps can remember the*
> *men who walked through the huts comforting others,*
> *giving away their last piece of bread. They may have*
> *been few in number but they offer sufficient proof that*
> *everything can be taken from a man, but one thing: the*
> *last of the human freedoms—to choose one's attitude in*
> *any given set of circumstances, to choose one's own way."*

This is the ultimate expression of values. To respond to any situation, however grave, in a way that is in line with what you value. It's not easy, but values aren't about the easy option. They are about what you want to stand for in this life.

Many years ago, when I was training to be a clinical psychologist, I worked on a team treating refugees with PTSD, just as I do now. I recall seeing a lady who had been through unspeakable cruelty and violence. I was shocked at what I had heard—sadly I hear it all the time now—and my supervisor had asked me to go with her the following week, a few days before Christmas, to an appointment with a psychiatrist to further explain her PTSD symptoms. I duly arrived and we attended the meeting. As we left, she stopped me and pulled a small package from her pocket and gave it to me. It was a present, rolled up in a little piece of paper. I opened it—it was a black hair clip, with some diamante decoration across it. She hardly knew any English. She had met me only once, yet she chose to act on her kindness. Despite her situation, despite how hard life was, despite how powerless she was, she chose to act on her values even when she must have felt so hopeless. I still have that hair clip to remind me that no matter what befalls you, you always have a choice about how you respond. If there are people in the world suffering unspeakable things who still choose to act on their values, then that path is open to all of us.

I know that some of you will think she only gave me that to get something from me. Maybe. I doubt it. The truth is, I don't know and nor do you. But I know what I choose to believe, and which thoughts empower me and make me more effective in the world. I find that people who are excessively cynical about other people's motives rarely do anything useful in improving the world. I'd rather believe in expressions of humanity than not. The world is full of terrible things. But it's also full of amazing acts of kindness and courage.

Values Are Always Accessible

The real beauty of values is that they are always accessible. You don't have to wait until you are richer, thinner, have a bigger house, better job, have more elegantly shaped eyebrows, straighter teeth, better behaved children, etc., before you can act on your values. You bring what you value to your actions straightaway. For example, if you value being curious and adventurous, you can start to plan your lone hike through the Amazon but you can also risk talking to a stranger when you go for lunch today. Is it the same as gliding down a river in a canoe hollowed out by your own hand using only the toothpick on your Swiss Army Knife? No. But talking to someone you don't know and stepping out of your comfort zone is part of being curious and adventurous—you are bringing those values into your life. If you want to go on really crazy adventures, buy a different sandwich for lunch. One you've *never* tried. Be bold. Chicken salad does not have to be your destiny.

What Values Are Not

Values Are Not Goals

We are a very goal-oriented society. Life is often about achieving the next goal on the list and getting a dopamine hit from the sense of achievement. We are hard-wired to seek out these rewards, which isn't a bad thing, of course, as it drives us forward. But without adding values into the mix, you are missing a trick. Unlike goals, values are not a destination you reach and then check off your list. Values are more like the direction you head in, like always heading east. Goals are the cities, trees, bridges, landmarks you pass by. You never arrive at "east" or any other point on your internal compass. The direction you choose in life is what guides, inspires and motivates you to keep moving forward. You might long for a promotion or to land a really good project or even just aspire to take control of an extra drawer in the office filing cabinet. But what happens when you achieve your goal? How do you want to behave when you get the thing you have always wanted? What values do you want to bring to your actions? How do you want to treat other people?

It's of note that studies looking at people who have had gastric sleeves for their obesity and return to a normal weight report increased levels of anxiety and depression despite achieving their goal. They became so fixated on achieving their goal that once they achieved it they didn't know what to do with themselves. The same is often true for people who have had plastic surgery. The question "now what?" looms large. Values provide a way to move forward and to maintain behavior changes. People who lose weight are more likely to maintain that behavior change and weight loss if they do it for themselves versus doing it because they think other people will treat them differently. In short, your intention is all-important—if you want to go to the gym more often, do it because you value being healthy not because it will get you into skinny jeans in two weeks. You might well achieve that goal, but you probably won't maintain the behaviors that got you there.

Values Are Not About Being Happy

I bet you don't want to hear that, but values are not just about feeling good, although of course a by-product of using your values to guide you can bring on the good times. It is not, however, always the case. Acting on your values can bring a lot of emotional pain. Treating refugees with PTSD means most of my day is spent hearing about torture, violence and the worst excesses of human nature. Does that make me feel happy like I do in Disneyland? No. But does it fit with my values of doing what I can to alleviate suffering? Yes, it does. It has meaning for me, inspiring and motivating me even when I do not feel like doing it. Not acting on values feels worse than acting on them, even when you just want to sit in bed all day eating chocolate.

If you are willing, try this exercise. Take a piece of paper and write down what's really important to you on one side—a person, pet, your job or something you love doing. Now turn the paper over. On the other side, write down what you fear about that. If what you fear is losing that person or activity, then you are not alone. It's what most people fear. Ask any parent what they fear most, and it's something happening to their child. For most people, the fear is losing the thing they really care about. As soon as you get really close to someone, you can lose them—parent, child, partner, friend, sibling. If there's something you love doing, there's always a risk you will lose the ability to do it. Here's the dilemma: are you willing to throw away the thing that you care about—being a loving parent, a brave water-skier, a compassionate colleague, a playful friend—in order to avoid the emotional pain that comes with caring about those things? I thought not. And in truth, it isn't possible to throw away one without the other. They are your hedgehogs. If you want the soft underbelly, you'll have to take the spiky parts, too.

All of us will experience emotional pain because we lose what we love. That's not something I can teach you how to change unless you are willing to live as an automaton. What is open to you, however, are the values you bring to these emotionally painful moments. How do you want to treat the friend who has had a cancer diagnosis? How do you want to comfort the parent coming to the end of their life? How do you want to treat yourself when you lose your job or when you can no longer do something you love? None of these things is "fun" or "pleasurable," but being present, open to your emotions and able to choose your values brings meaning to life.

Values Are Not Rules

Don't let "should" or "must" hijack your values. There are no right or wrong values either. Values need to be held lightly, and used as gentle guides nudging you in the right direction, like a friendly golden retriever. They are not sticks to beat yourself with. You won't always be able to act on your values in the way that you want. Furthermore, values will sometimes need prioritizing as they may conflict. Maybe you value being a good friend but prioritize a work project over a night out because you also value being conscientious. Sometimes you will have to prioritize values that may not be compatible at that moment. That doesn't mean that the value you don't prioritize disappears forever. Think of your values as countries on a globe: when you look at Mexico you cannot, at the same time, see the Democratic Republic of Congo. The DRC is still there; you are just choosing to focus on Central America right now. The same is true of your values. You might focus on being a loving parent and spending time with your kids rather than on expressing your creativity by building the Parthenon out of matchsticks at a particular moment. Your creativity is still there; it's just not what you want to focus on right now.

The Revenge of Your Mind

Why have I been asking you to defuse from thoughts, make room for feelings you don't want and ramp up your mindfulness? Not just for kicks, but because the second you start moving toward addressing some big values questions, your mind is going to have something to say about it, and feelings of sadness, guilt, shame, fear of failure, along with their other pals, will show up and throw you off track just when you are getting to the good part.

Have you seen *The Karate Kid*? If yes, you'll understand where I am going with this. If no, then here's a summary (and seriously, where have you been?): In short, lonely kid Danny goes to wise, old Mr. Miyagi to learn karate to defend himself from the school bullies. Mr. Miyagi agrees to teach him, but much to Danny's frustration Mr. Miyagi only gives him chores to do: painting a fence, waxing the fence. Not taking kindly to being exploited for his free labor, Danny confronts Mr. Miyagi—he wants to learn the moves, not DIY. Mr. Miyagi, who is very wise (we know this because he doesn't say much and nods sagely a lot), tells him that he is learning karate. He tells Danny, "Brush up!" and Danny performs the action—it is a karate move! Who knew? "Wax on! Wax off"—Danny mimics the action of waxing the fence, and it's another karate move! He's been getting the moves without realizing it! Danny is like you, and I am like Mr. Miyagi but less wise and sage, plus, also, I talk a lot more. Defusion, expansion, mindfulness and perspective-taking are the moves I have shown you, the ninja skills you need to move forward to the next level. Now you are ready to play the game, reader-san. And the game is all about values.

Identifying Your Values

Now that you have the lowdown on values and the skills to deal with the inevitable barriers your mind will throw up, it's time to start finding out what matters to you. Here's a selection of exercises you can return to repeatedly to orient yourself and bring some meaning to proceedings.

Acceptance	Adventure	Affection
Assertiveness	Beauty	Belonging
Caring	Compassion	Conformity
Connection	Conscientiousness	Courage
Creativity	Curiosity	Dedication
Discipline	Equality	Excitement
Experience	Fairness	Faith
Fitness	Freedom	Friendliness
Fun	Generosity	Gratitude
Health	Honesty	Humor
Independence	Integrity	Justice
Kindness	Knowledge	Leadership
Learning	Love	Loyalty
Openness	Organization	Patience
Peace	Playfulness	Power
Reliability	Respect	Risk
Security	Self-Awareness	Sensuality
Sociability	Spontaneity	Spirituality
Tolerance	Trust	Wisdom

Choosing Your Values

On this page is a list of commonly held values. It is by no means exhaustive, so feel free to add your own. Read through the list and mark the ones that feel important to you. Then try to pick out the five that are the most important to you. Now you can start thinking about whether you are expressing these values in your life and what behaviors you would be doing if you were using your values as a compass. Maybe there are some values you'd like to try on, like a new coat, in which case go ahead and see what fits. You can always return it if it turns out to be like that oversize asymmetrical shirt/furry mules/other ill-advised fashion fail you have been known to indulge in.

Areas of Life	Values I want to show
Family	
Intimate Relationships	
Children	
Friends/Social Life	
Work/Career	
Education/Learning	
Leisure/Recreation	
Spirituality/Religion	
Citizenship/Community Life	
Health (physical and mental)	
Art/Creativity	

*Inspired by "Areas of Life" from Kelly Wilson's *The Valued Living Questionnaire*, 2002

Now that you have thought a bit more about your values, you can start clarifying areas of life where you would like to show these values by using the table on this page. Some of these areas of life may not be important to you at all, and if I have missed out any, feel free to add your own.

Now We Are Eighty. Or Thirty. Or Fifty.

This is a nice exercise to bring values to life (Harris 2008). Close your eyes and imagine vividly in your head that you are at a party for a milestone birthday in the future. You are looking back on your life as it is today. Complete the following sentences:

- I spent too much time worrying about . . .
- I spent too little time doing things such as . . .
- If I could go back in time, then what I would do differently from today onward is . . .
- I would spend more time . . .
- I would tell myself . . .

Attending Your Own Funeral

Bronnie Ware, a palliative care nurse, collated the five most common regrets of the dying. This is what people say they regret most as they come to the end of their lives:

- I wish I'd had the courage to live a life true to myself, not the life others expected of me.
- I wish I hadn't worked so hard.
- I wish I'd had the courage to express my feelings.
- I wish I had stayed in touch with my friends.
- I wish that I had let myself be happier.

Those were the regrets of people who couldn't turn things around, but you can. Focus on what matters most to you now, whether you are eighteen or eighty.

This exercise will help you work out what you really care about. Attending Your Own Funeral (Hayes & Smith 2005) is not as grim as it sounds. In fact, I would say that this is one of the most powerful and life-affirming exercises you can do. I would give yourself some time alone to do it when you are not going to be disturbed. It can be an emotional and moving experience. By the end of it, I think you will have a much better sense of what you want your life to be about.

Imagine that you have died. You've lived a good life, one in which your values guided, motivated and inspired you. Imagine that somehow you are able to watch your own funeral service. Three people stand up to give a eulogy about you—they are three people from different spheres of your life: family members, colleagues, friends—it can be anyone you like, but just try to have the different areas of your life represented. You can even do this for relationships that don't yet exist—what you would want a child or partner to say about you even if you don't have that person in your life yet.

As each one gives their speech, vividly imagine what you would like each person to say about you. See if you can see their expressions and hear their voices. Notice how you feel in your body as you hear them talk about what you stood for in life, about what you meant to them, about the things you did that were a true reflection of you and your values. You can be bold here; don't hold back. Try to connect deeply with what you want your loved ones to say.

Once you have done this, perhaps ask yourself who you wanted to speak at the funeral. What words did they use to talk about you? Are those words clues to what you value? Did you feel a gap between what you wanted them to say about your life and how you are living your life now? This exercise reveals what sort of person you truly want to be. What are the barriers to you living your life as that kind of person right now?

It's powerful, no? And perhaps painful, too, especially if you feel you are far from being the kind of person you want to be and doing the kinds of things you want to do. This pain tells you what really matters to you. Don't push that away, but use it like a lighthouse to guide you to a more meaningful, fulfilling and vital life.

A Values Letter

Writing about values has a bigger effect on behavior than just choosing values from a list. To engage with your values a bit more, give yourself ten minutes (set a timer) to write about a value you really care about, perhaps one you have already identified from earlier exercises. Here are some prompts to get you going:

- Which area of life do I care about showing this value in?
- Has there been a time in my life when this value has been important?
- Have there been times when I stepped away from this value? How did I behave at those times? Did it cost me anything?
- When have I shown behaviors in line with this value? What did that feel like?
- Have I acted on this value in the past even if it was hard?
- If I wanted to act on this value more in my life, what behaviors would I have to show?

Secret Values

The first rule of Secret Values (Hayes 2019) is you don't talk about Secret Values. Total secrecy is key. Sign the Official Values Secrecy Act. Don't crack under interrogation. Choose a value and then plot ways to act on it without anyone knowing. Leave a present for a friend without saying it was you, give money to a charity anonymously, be kind to a stranger just because you value kindness. The important point is that you are doing it because your values are intrinsically rewarding, not because you are hoping for praise or approval from others. This is a great way to find out what matters to you without muddying the waters with what other people think. Tell no one.

The Problem Vacuum Cleaner

Imagine that I have a vacuum cleaner that sucks up all the things that stand in your way. I come over to your place with my newly patented device and start my psychological vacuuming (maybe this sounds weird, on reflection). You no longer worry about what other people think; painful thoughts, memories, feelings and physical sensations are like water off a very zen duck's back; you have all the money you need—you zip off on luxury safari holidays, buy cars with leather interiors and shop daily from the finest range in your local supermarket without an iota of concern for your bank balance. Now, what will you do with your time? Think about how you will spend your day now that you are totally free to choose. Imagine I follow you around filming you and getting on your nerves. What would I actually see you doing now that you don't have any obstacles?

Sweet Moments

Try this exercise (Wilson & Dufrene 2009), and think back to a moment in your life when you felt alive, vital, fulfilled. Bring this memory to life vividly, focusing not only on what you see and hear in that memory but also on what you can smell, touch, taste and feel in your body. What were you doing in that sweet moment? Who was with you? Where were you? Did you notice how present you were in that moment? See if you can tap into what you feel in your body, not just what your mind says.

Ask yourself what it was about that moment that was so special to you. What values were in play? What does this moment tell you about what you care about?

BOTTOM LINE

Human beings long for meaning in life to sustain and connect us with what matters. Focusing on what you really want to stand for will give you a strong sense of meaning where it may previously have been lacking. Now you can raise your head up from the daily grind to answer the biggest questions life throws at you: who do you want to be, where do you want to go and how do you want to get there? Values will give you a way to answer these questions, not by showing you the meaning *of* life, but by showing you the meaning *in* life.

Chapter 7
How to Take Action

"Change your life today. Don't gamble on the
future, act now, without delay."

—SIMONE DE BEAUVOIR

All of this is just an intellectual exercise if you don't take action. Maybe the chapters so far have given you a moment of chin-rubbing insight, but nothing will change in the fabric of your life if you don't do something differently. This is how to take meaningful, committed action.

Why We Start Off on the Wrong Foot

Research shows that most people give up their New Year's resolutions by January 19. So, that's a total of only eighteen days spent trying to do something differently. Or put another way, you spend only 5 percent of the year sticking to a change and 95 percent of it berating yourself for not sticking to it or wishing your life looked different. It's hardly surprising that the wheels come off; setting goals or making resolutions is the easy part, but without the psychological flexibility skills of defusion, acceptance, mindfulness, values and committed action, you are flying blind. It looks like this:

Try to change behavior without a plan → Feel unmotivated + self-criticize → Give up → Nothing changes

There's nothing to guide you and nothing to help you deal with the tricky moments when things start going pear-shaped. It isn't hard to see, for example, how quickly you will ditch a goal to lose weight if:

1. You fuse with thoughts like "It's too hard" or "I am too stressed to do it now" or "I fell off the wagon so there's no point continuing. Pass me more eclairs. And a doughnut."
2. You are not willing to experience the unwanted feelings that come with doing something challenging.
3. You aren't clear about your values and why you want to lose weight.
4. You don't know how to make habits stick or to set goals and so you give up.

You now know how to manage 1, 2 and 3. Now we need to move on to 4. Sorry? What's that you say? Oh, you have sort of been paying attention but you had some mind-wandering problems? Ah, attention is the scarcest of human resources these days. I invite you to return to the previous chapters: How to Think Better, How to Feel Better, How to Have Perspective and How to Be Right Here, Right Now (so basically all of it), before you really get into the nuts and bolts of taking action in your life; otherwise you are setting yourself up for disappointment. If, however, you are just window shopping through this chapter, then feel free to browse and check out the wares.

Why You Keep Making the Same Mistakes

Before we go any further, I want to share with you the life-changing magic of behavioral analysis (Skinner 1953). In short, I am going to show you why you keep finding yourself in the same old patterns, doing the same old thing. If you've ever spent an hour or two hunched over, chin resting on fist, deep in thought like a beardy Greek philosopher asking yourself, "Why? Why? Why can I never do things differently? Why isn't life panning out the way I want despite my best efforts? Where did this beard come from?", then this is for you.

Every behavior you do has a purpose or intention, whether or not you are aware of it. Pretty often, we are not aware of the reasons we do something and why we persist in doing it. In order to figure out our patterns of behavior, we need to understand antecedents, behaviors and consequences.

Antecedents: antecedents are triggers or stimuli. They are what immediately precede a behavior. They can be situations, thoughts, feelings or physical sensations.

Behavior: the behavior is anything that you do. Behaviors can be observable behaviors, e.g., drinking, watching TV, eating, staring at the wall, plucking chin hairs. They are things that can be "observed" even if you do them alone. Behaviors can also be private or internal, e.g., ruminating, self-talk, worrying, fantasizing. You can be doing them, but they cannot be easily observed by another person.

Consequences: these are the events that immediately follow the behavior and that lead to it persisting or increasing.

So what does this look like in real life? Imagine that you are very unhappy in your job. It pays the bills but you have to drag your sorry self there every day. You spend a lot of time looking at other career options (opening a bookshop, becoming an acrobat, retraining as a podiatrist, etc.), but none of it gets very far. In order to deal with your frustration you drink more than you should, stay home watching TV and avoid anyone who makes you feel like a failure. You feel an ongoing lack of purpose and meaning. Cripes. What's to be done? As with all problems, put it into an ABC (antecedents, behaviors, consequence) table, like the one shown on the next page.

Antecedent	Behavior	Consequence
Situation *Thoughts* *Feelings* *Physical sensations* *Urges*	*What you do!*	*Consequences of your response*
Situation: terrible day at work Thoughts: I will never leave there. I can't stand it Feelings: anxiety Physical sensations: heart races, muscles tense, feel sick Urges: urge to get rid of these feelings	Drink Binge-watch TV Avoid friends who have better jobs	Immediate: relief!!! I don't have to deal with it, and horrible feelings and thoughts go away. Alcohol numbs me. I forget about the problem for a bit. Long-term: no change in my situation Not living a life in line with values The same things keep happening and another year passes

Don't columns and rows make it all better? The key point to take away is that all behaviors have reinforcing consequences that mean that behavior is likely to persist. In this instance, the reinforcing consequence is the relief you feel when you drink to get rid of feelings of anxiety. Hooray! It's gone! What's the problem?! All is dandy! Not so fast, muchacha. Look what lurks in the lower levels of your consequences column. The long term. In reinforcing-consequences terms, it's the boring cousin, whereas imme-diate consequences are like your super-fun cousin who al-ways knows the best bars. When we are on autopilot, we are primarily concerned with feeling better, getting rid of thoughts and feelings we don't want or escaping from a sit-uation we don't like. We are not focused on what the long-term, unintended consequences of our behaviors are: a life not in tune with personal values and a lack of purpose and meaning.

How Not to Make the Same Mistakes

So now you know. You keep doing the same old things because it takes away your pain in the short term—which you are probably well aware of with some behaviors, al-though less so with others—and every time this happens it makes it more likely it will happen yet again unless you *consciously* do something about it. The first step is to re-spond differently to your antecedents or triggers by defus-ing from thoughts and opening up to feelings using the psychological flexibility skills you have already learned. Take a look at the table on page 121 to see how this works. Once you can do this, you open up a whole new column on your behavior analysis table. That's some valuable real estate right there with a serious amount of brain space. It's the psychological equivalent of a five-bedroom house with a garden, pool and parking in Central London. Now you can think about the next column: Values-Driven Behaviors—actions you can take which are a) in line with your values and b) will make meaningful, concrete changes to your life. In this instance it might be about setting goals to move jobs but it really could be anything which is in line with your values. Values are often the missing component when people come to take action. It's pretty hard, though not impossible, to stick to new behaviors if there aren't values involved. You can do it, but you are reliant on external rewards which are not always in your control. If you do something in line with your values, you have intrinsic rewards because you commit to a course of action because it matters to you. You are always in control of those actions whether there is some external reward or not.

Now you have got yourself some well-needed space to take new actions, choose one domain of life in which to make changes, e.g., work, health, relationships, education, community, social. Don't choose more than one or you will spread yourself too thin. The aim of all new behaviors is to turn them into habits which is considerably harder if you are trying to do it across several areas of your life. If you want to really make a change, cut down on empty commitments which drain your time and energy. Focus on what matters. Next, think about the values you want to show in this area of your life. Done that? Written it down? (Always write it down.) OK, now you're good to go.

Get SMART

Setting goals that are SMART (specific, meaningful, achievable, realistic and time-framed) increases the likelihood of achieving those goals (Doran 1981).

Specific: Be clear about what actions you are going to take, when you are going to take them and where. Saying I am going to get fitter isn't a goal. It's a vague pipe dream. A goal would be I will walk up the stairs to my office three days this week, on Monday, Wednesday and Friday. It needs to be specific so you are clear about what you are going to do when the time comes. Reduce the need for unnecessary decision-making, and therefore the option to talk yourself out of it, when you are trying to achieve a goal or start a habit by pre-deciding your action plan. Before long, these little actions become habits you don't have to think about.

Meaningful: goals should be guided by our values and have meaning. Are your goals yours or someone else's?

Achievable: do you currently have the resources and capabilities to achieve this goal? If not, what do you need to do or what needs to happen to make this goal achievable?

Realistic: given the competing demands in your life, such as health, time and finances, is this goal

Antecedent	Behavior		Values-Driven Behavior	Consequence
Situation *Thoughts* *Feelings* *Physical sensations* *Urges*	*What you do!*		*Also stuff you do!*	*Consequences of your response*
Situation: terrible day at work Thoughts: I will never leave there. I can't stand it Feelings: anxiety Physical sensations: heart races, muscles tense, feel sick Urges: Urge to get rid of these feelings	Defusion Acceptance Mindfulness	SPACE AND CHOICE Spread your arms out, revel in the space in your head to make different choices	Set goals Solve problems Make mindful decisions	Immediate: more control over autopilot actions Long-term: work toward finding a new job Live my values while in my current job Look after my health

realistic? Or do you need to set another, more
realistic goal?

Time-Framed: be crystal clear about what you are
going to do and when you are going to do it in
order to increase the likelihood of you achieving
your goal. Select a time and date by which you
want to achieve this goal.

Goals Don't Necessarily Lead To Happiness

Goal setting needs to come with a health warning in our
achievement-driven society. If you just set goals for the sake
of achieving goals, then life will ultimately lack the purpose
and meaning you might be craving—checking off goal after
goal, seductive though it is, won't ultimately give you what
you are after. Also beware predicting that when you achieve
your goal or get what you want, you'll feel happy. That kind
of thinking really pulls you out of the present and away from
the satisfaction of being able to act on your values right now.
Defuse from those thoughts and focus as much on the process and the values you want to show as the things you want
to achieve. How you do it counts as much as what you do.

Hack Your Environment

Behavior change is hard. Make your environment and
the systems around you work to your advantage to create

ongoing progress. If you want to reduce a bad habit, then make it harder for yourself to do it. Want to spend less time scrolling mindlessly on your phone? Have a place by the front door where you leave it to charge. Want to watch less TV? Put the remote controls in a drawer and unplug the TV from the wall. If you want to introduce a new habit, make it easier for yourself to do it. Need to get to the gym more? Leave your gym bag packed and ready by the front door. If you want to eat more healthily, make healthy food visible and accessible. Hide the cookies in some Tupperware at the back of the cupboard under the jar of preserved lemons you never use. Reduce all unnecessary obstacles to healthy eating by putting your chopped carrots front and center of your fridge. If you are tired and cranky, eating healthily is not going to happen if you have to go out to the supermarket to buy quinoa and eggplants or some such. Nor will you go for a run if you have to spend twenty minutes looking for your sports bra. Reduce obstacles to habits you want and add obstacles to habits you don't want.

Hook Your Habits

If you want to introduce a new habit, then let it hook onto an already established habit (Fogg 2020). Keen to do more squats? Plan to do it after you brush your teeth. Want to call your elderly Aunt Adele every week? Stack it onto your Saturday morning run. Work out your current habits that can serve as triggers—getting up, brushing your teeth, showering, drinking coffee or tea, getting your bag ready for work, switching on your computer, traveling to and from work, taking your coat off when you get home, etc. You get the idea. Make a list of what you habitually do and then stack a new habit onto it to give yourself the best chance of doing it.

The Myth of Motivation

Motivation and willpower are psychological red herrings. They are internal feelings that come and go just as every feeling and physical sensation ebbs and flows. They may or may not be present when you need to take action, which can leave you rather high and dry. Relying on internal states to decide whether or not you take meaningful action is as random as saying you'll do something only if the clouds you see in the sky that day are in the shape of pineapples.

Instead of being at the mercy of whether you feel like it or not, revel in the fact that you are not a slave to your thoughts. You can prove to yourself right now that you are always in control of your actions no matter what your mind tells you. Tell yourself repeatedly that you cannot lift up your left leg. Doing it? Good. Now keep saying, "I can't lift up my left leg. I can't and I won't. So there." Now lift up your left leg. See how you are doing one thing with your body while telling yourself you both cannot and will not do it? You have control over what you do with your arms and legs and what you say despite what your mind would have you believe. If you are saying, "Of course I can do that. This is a foolish exercise," then ask yourself this: when your mind says for the third time this week, "You know what? Don't take the stairs today, just wait till you have a bit more energy. You can do it tomorrow instead," do you head up those stairs because fitness is important to you or do you avoid it, wait for the lift and get some short-term relief? Thought so. You can put your leg down now. We are all, at one time or another, under the control of the dictates from our minds despite wanting to make changes in our lives. Next time you want to achieve an important, values-based goal and your mind says, "I don't wanna!" with its bottom lip sticking out, remember you can defuse from that thought and be in control of your actions. If lifting up your leg helps you to remember this, then hop on.

Just Show Up a Little Bit a Lot of the Time

Small, consistent behavior is more important in achieving goals and making progress than one grand gesture. You need to show up a little bit a lot of the time to succeed. Making small, easy and quick changes today won't get you big results tomorrow. But doing it a bit each day will. Eating less sugar today will make little difference to your weight tomorrow. Reducing your sugar intake a little bit every day will. Running ten minutes today will not improve your fitness tomorrow either. But run ten minutes every day for a month, and you will notice a change. One of the main reasons people don't achieve their goals is that they make them too hard and overextend themselves too early in the process. When you start with a new goal, ask yourself what's the easiest, peasiest step you can start with. Make it as easy as jumping off a piece of paper on the floor. Persist with the small, easy changes for the big results. Every step, every shuffle or limp forward, is still progress. Don't forget your reinforcing consequences either: the more likely you are to succeed at each step, the likelier you are to keep going. Small goals like this allow you to keep calibrating and recalibrating your behaviors to keep you heading in the right direction.

What You Track Is What You Change

You need to keep tracking and monitoring your progress to see if you are making changes. The easiest way to do this is to set up something on your phone using a simple note-taking app. Don't get distracted by needing something with lots of bells and whistles, just start simply for now. If you have identified creativity as a value and have set yourself the target of drawing once a week for forty-five minutes, note down afterward what you were able to achieve. If you weren't able to do anything this week, then make your goal easier and just try for fifteen minutes and make sure you are setting SMART goals and making your environment work for you. If you did forty-five minutes, then you can recalibrate and set a different goal for the following week, perhaps an hour. Omitting measuring your progress will often lead to giving up altogether because your goal is either too easy or too hard. Tracking allows you to get some immediate feedback to reinforce your efforts.

Fall Down. Lick Wounds. Get Up. Move Forward a Little Bit. Repeat.

You will have days or weeks when you don't take action. You will have days when you feel like you have failed and giving up altogether feels enormously appealing. But you've been there and done that, and now you want to do it differently. You want—gulp—some actual resilience. Well, first off, resilience is not a thing you have. It's the process of getting back up. It isn't the absence of sadness, fear or anxiety. It's having all those things and taking them forward with you.

The root of resilience comes from the Latin word *resiliere* (hi there, Latin fans!) which means "to spring back." It does not mean to never ever fall down under any circumstances. Falling down is going to be part of it if you want to live a rich and meaningful life. Throughout this book you have been learning the psychological flexibility skills to deal with thoughts and feelings that come when things inevitably go awry. Employing these skills will allow you the space to figure out where you went off track, and the tools in this chapter will show you how to keep moving forward. It should start to look a bit like this:

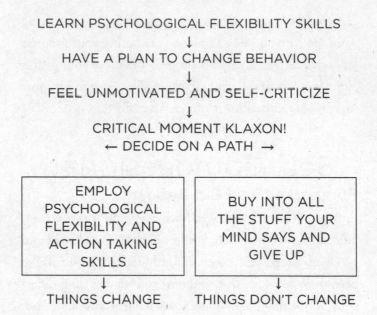

LEARN PSYCHOLOGICAL FLEXIBILITY SKILLS
↓
HAVE A PLAN TO CHANGE BEHAVIOR
↓
FEEL UNMOTIVATED AND SELF-CRITICIZE
↓
CRITICAL MOMENT KLAXON!
← DECIDE ON A PATH →

EMPLOY PSYCHOLOGICAL FLEXIBILITY AND ACTION TAKING SKILLS	BUY INTO ALL THE STUFF YOUR MIND SAYS AND GIVE UP
↓	↓
THINGS CHANGE	THINGS DON'T CHANGE

In the end, if you keep using the skills you have learned, things will change. The key is understanding that psychological flexibility comes first. Change will follow.

BOTTOM LINE

Understanding your self-defeating and self-limiting patterns will allow you to make different, broader choices in your life that are much more aligned with your values and with what you really care about. Keep coming back to all the skills you have learned, keep your eye on the long term, put your values front and center and you will take small steps toward big changes.

Chapter 8

How to Be Self-Compassionate

"Sometimes I lie awake at night and I ask, 'Why me?' then a voice answers 'Nothing personal, your name just happened to come up.'"

—CHARLIE BROWN

Emotional pain is universal. Working with refugees teaches me daily that bad things happen to good people for no rhyme or reason. We don't choose the brains and bodies we are born with, and we don't choose the suffering that life can dole out.

Self-compassion has long been a cornerstone of Buddhism and other religious and spiritual traditions, but in recent years it has started to form an important part of science-based treatments for a range of psychological difficulties. If you want to embrace a totally new way of relating to yourself and others that can significantly improve your life, then read on. It's time to start showing some passion for self-compassion.

What Is It?

Self-compassion is a way of relating to yourself with kindness, warmth and affection in the face of your suffering. It's about showing the same compassion to yourself you would show to a friend who was suffering. Its benefits are striking: a robust body of research shows that people who are self-compassionate experience less psychological distress, greater resilience in the face of life's many ups and downs and report higher levels of life satisfaction. And it benefits those around you too—research shows that people with higher levels of self-compassion display more positive relationship behavior than those who have low self-compassion. Self-compassion is basically a psychological superpower that is yours for the taking. The great news is that self-compassion isn't a trait you either have or don't, like toenails that grow weirdly or blue eyes—it's something you can actually teach yourself.

According to one of the world's leading self-compassion researchers, Kristin Neff, self-compassion is made up of three distinct but interacting elements (Neff 2003a): self-kindness, common humanity and mindfulness.

- **Self-kindness** (as opposed to self-criticism) is the tendency in individuals to treat themselves with understanding and care rather than being self-critical or judgmental.
- **Common humanity** (as opposed to isolation) involves recognizing that *we all fail*, make mistakes and that we are not alone in our suffering.
- **Mindfulness** (as opposed to overidentification), as you now know, involves being aware of the present moment. It allows you to step back and take a nonjudgmental perspective on yourself and your life.

So those are three elements of self-compassion; so far, so good. But to proceed further in your self-compassion quest, you've got to know what operating system your brain is running so you can work with it, not against it. The first step is to understand that your brain is basically running three types of emotion regulation systems (Depue & Morrone-Strupinsky 2005; Gilbert 2009): the threat and protection system; the drive, resource-seeking and excitement system; and the contentment and soothing system. Understanding these systems, how they work and what happens when they are activated, is a crucial first step in developing self-compassion. Otherwise you're going to be as frustrated as a Mac user trying to use a Windows operating system. And there's nothing more frustrating than not understanding your computer.

Threat system: this is where your fight-or-flight system resides. It's what comes online when you run away from danger (muggers, snakes, people to whom you owe large sums of money) or fight back. The aim of the threat system is to alert you to life-threatening danger to your physical integrity. The kinds of emotions you feel when the threat system is activated are anxiety, anger and disgust.

When your threat system is active, your motivations are to stay alive and to protect yourself—and consequently the brain organizes what you pay attention to (there's something with big teeth rustling in that corner), what you think (doom is but a second away!), what you do (run or fight or freeze), what images and memories are present (vividly seeing yourself being savaged by your predator), what your body does (prepares to run or fight, so your heart will beat faster, you will feel short of breath and your muscles will tense) and what threat-based emotions you feel (anxiety).

This threat system is very easy to trigger, like poking a crocodile on the nose with a big stick, and it's what has helped us survive. The problem now is that this system is activated not just by threats to our physical self but also by threats to our self-concept. This can come from external sources such as others being cruel and critical, but it can also be triggered by your own self-criticism and self-attack. You can quite literally make yourself feel under threat by your self-talk.

Studies using Functional Magnetic Resonance Imaging (imaging techniques that measure activity in the brain) show that your brain responds in a similar way to self-generated threats, like self-criticism, as it does to criticism from someone else or indeed to an actual threat to your physical integrity. It's like it cannot tell the difference between what you yourself generate and what is actually out there in real life. It will result in similar physiological reactions—racing heart, tense muscles, knots in your stomach—even though you just thought it all up yourself. Isn't that something? You can actually stimulate your own threat system (which will then influence your emotions, thoughts, motivations and actions) by being nasty to yourself. And there's precious little opportunity to choose valued actions when you are operating only from within your threat system.

While threats to our physical selves activate the threat system, so do social threats. We have evolved to fear being rejected because it means we could be thrown out of the group, and we are primarily social beings. Shame, and its cousins embarrassment and humiliation, are all threat-based emotions. They can only be experienced in the context of other people: shame only works because we feel worthless in the eyes of others, which, over time, results in feeling worthless in ourselves.

The dangers of social rejection from the group in the early days of our evolution meant DOOM. You couldn't trudge through harsh tundras thousands of years ago and survive without the help of others—you wouldn't be able to get enough food or protect yourself from threats, especially if you were injured, or caring for offspring. So now when you criticize yourself and overthink, your brain goes into threat mode, as it is programmed to, and releases cortisol and adrenaline to prod you into action. That's fine if the threat is short-lived and you can quickly return your system to normal. But when the threat system is constantly activated, as it is in modern life through a thousand daily moments of stress, the result is a constant release of adrenaline and cortisol, which has significant negative effects on our psychological and physical well-being. It's what we think of as chronic stress.

Drive system: this is your achieving system, which stimulates you to get things like food, shelter, sex, friendship. It's also what is at play when you seek out a promotion at work, a new house, a state-of-the-art food processor—whatever your thing is, really. It's about wanting, striving and achieving; the emotions you'll find here are things like pleasure, fun or excitement. Again, not unhelpful in our evolution, but our modern-day focus on these elements breeds much dissatisfaction. Our society values being competitive and aggressively invites you to compare yourself with others, which, of course, is heightened by social media.

And when we get what we want or strive for—jobs, sex, houses, likes, money—we get a nice little dopamine boost, a buzz that is so very reinforcing. Sometimes (alright, frequently) you might try to regulate the unpleasant feelings from your threat system by seeking status or material possessions. The problem with this as your only response to your threat system is twofold. Firstly, it works in the short term but there are only so many food processors you can buy before you start yearning for something more meaningful. Secondly, if you don't achieve what you strive for, you feel inadequate, fear the threat of social rejection and so do what you know best—criticize yourself further and feed your threat system even more. Which you then try to deal with by going back to the drive system for answers. Put aggressive advertising into the mix, and it's hardly surprising that we are on a treadmill of trying to get more and more yet never generate the feelings of peace, contentment and self-acceptance we crave. If this sounds like you, it's probably because you are bouncing and rebounding only between your threat system and your drive system and wondering why you have so many kitchen appliances.

Soothing system: this is the system where the magic lies but that no one has ever heard of. This system is linked to feelings of soothing and contentment and, crucially, safeness. It's about non-wanting and about being OK where you are. Sounds nice, no? Don't you like the idea of "non-wanting"?

The soothing system is the result of our evolution as mammals. Mammals show care and affection to their offspring, which is markedly different to reptiles, who just slither off leaving their little'uns to figure it out for themselves, although of course we were reptiles once, too. The threat system, with its emphasis on survival, is the reptilian part of our brain. However, as mammals, we learn to generate feelings of safeness and contentment from our caregivers, who soothe and comfort us with touch, gentle voices and warmth. The loss of human touch for many during the pandemic has been profound, and with good reason—we are programmed to need it. It is this mammalian caregiving that activates our soothing system and the release of oxytocin. It is from this place of emotional safeness that we can thrive and make better use of our drive systems.

Activating the soothing system allows space and time to "rest and digest." Other mammals rest and digest following stress (running away from predators), which allows the body to repair. An antelope who has recently survived an attack from a lion will have experienced a huge fight-or-flight response, but soon after the danger has gone, you will see her resting and digesting, chewing away on grass, perhaps having a little drink at a local watering hole. Her body is repairing itself. The antelope does not have conversations with her best friend antelope about why the lion attacked her, why she was such a loser for running away and whether it will happen again tomorrow. The antelope is not judging her behavior and then criticizing herself for it—this is a uniquely human ability that keeps our threat system active. In short, we keep making it worse for ourselves.

It's at moments of self-attack, and indeed emotional attack from others, that we need to move beyond using only the drive system to tone down our threat system. We need to find a balance among all three systems to thrive, and activating the soothing system with some self-compassion moves is just the thing.

It's Complicated

Things are made trickier by the fact that we have these "new brain" capabilities. These are the bits of our brains that can fantasize, plan and imagine. You'll recall from "Brain 101" that this is what makes us uniquely human. However, in conjunction with our emotion regulation systems, it has the potential for great acts of humanity but also great cruelty. The ability to think up terrible things to do to people, and to plan them and carry them out is the amalgamation of anger in the threat-based system with the planning capabilities of our new mind. It never ceases to horrify me when I hear what torturers around the world come up with. And at the same time the stories of incredible humanity, resilience and kindness never fail to inspire me. Human beings are capable of both terrible cruelty and astonishing kindness—both of these depend on how we choose to work with our brains, emotions and motivations. Maybe we cannot eradicate all the darkness in the world, but perhaps we can, at least, increase the light. Understanding how we operate is a first step toward that.

You Didn't Choose Your Programming

The key thing to know about these emotion regulation systems is this: You. Did. Not. Choose. Them. They, like the rest of your brain and body, were baked into you from the start. It's not your fault you have all this tricky wiring and programming in your body and brain. They are the result of our evolution. Now, you can't change your operating system entirely, but you can change how you respond to it through the self-awareness capabilities of your new brain so that you can choose different behaviors and break unhelpful and harmful patterns that may be causing you, and others, undue suffering. In short, you can learn to work with the way your mind operates, not against it. That, my friend, is liberating.

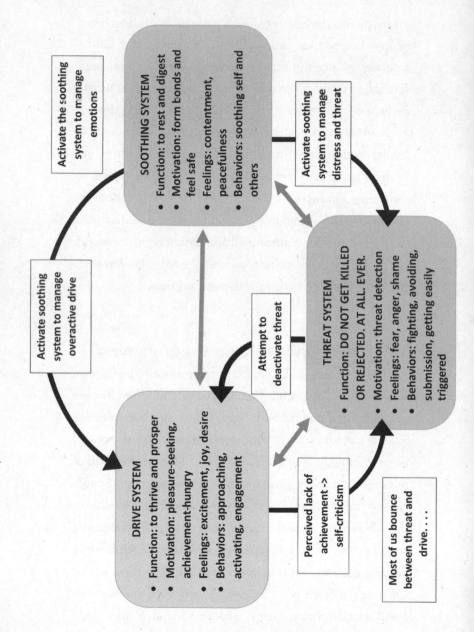

Self-Compassion Myths

Do you think compassion is a good thing? Is it something that helps? What role has compassion played in this COVID-19 crisis? I am guessing you judge it to be a fine thing and are thinking of the work of healthcare professionals, among others, strapped into PPE doing their utmost to care for the sick and dying. Now, what do you think of self-compassion? What comes to mind? I suspect a number of you are experiencing a strong sensation of toe-curling cringiness at the thought of self-compassion. Isn't it just massive self-indulgence? I must admit that, in the past, I would have been all like, "This is all woo-woo candles, rose petal baths and giving myself face massages while the world goes to hell in a handbasket" and turned my smug nose up at it. But that's before I found out what it actually was, that there is robust evidence that it can make a profound difference in people's lives; I liked it so much that I wrote my doctoral thesis on it. There's nothing like writing a thesis on something to make you hate it with a venom reserved only for perpetrators of war crimes and people who don't move along the platform in tube stations, but it's to self-compassion's credit that I still think it's a great thing and would happily and graciously invite it over for tea.

Nonetheless, I know how easy it is to be suspicious of things that sound a little, you know, umm, alternative, so I am going to dispel some myths for you.

Self-Compassion Is Not Self-Indulgence

One of the main reasons people aren't self-compassionate is that they are afraid they will become self-indulgent, lose all motivation and find themselves sitting in their pants on the sofa in the middle of the day picking yesterday's takeout from their unbrushed teeth while their kids forage for cigarette butts in the neighbors' bins. But the truth is quite different—self compassion and self-indulgence are two very different things.

Rarely would we try to encourage someone to do their best by criticizing them, something most parents know. Telling your kids to suck it up and do better when you find them howling their eyes out after failing to get into the woodwind section of the school orchestra or being left out of the tiddlywinks squad with regional championships round the corner will not motivate them in any sort of long-term or sustainable way. Yes, of course, some people will respond and "pull it out of the bag," finding themselves puffing away on their clarinet in front of the whole school while you beam smugly, but it will come at the cost of them learning to motivate themselves, their relationship with themselves and probably their relationship with you. If that all sounds a bit wishy-washy for you, then take it from the mighty Sir Alex Ferguson, famous for managing Manchester United during their greatest years (I stand by this, don't write in to tell me otherwise) and also famous for being quite shouty and not a big softy. This is what he says about how to motivate people: "No one likes to be criticized. Few people get better with criticism; most respond to encouragement instead. So I tried to give encouragement when I could. For a player—for any human being—there is nothing better than hearing 'Well done.' Those are the two best words ever invented."

So if you, and Sir Alex, wouldn't use criticism to motivate others, then why would you do it to yourself? I suspect because it works some of the time (think back to reinforcing consequences in chapter 7) and because it's what you've learned to do and the alternative—being self-compassionate—feels indulgent. At worst, you might not even try to challenge yourself lest you unleash a volley of self-criticism in the event of failure. The research and science speak volumes on this front: self-compassionate people aim just as high as those who are not self-compassionate but aren't as distressed and frustrated if they don't reach their goals (Neff 2003a); self-compassion is also linked to adaptive ways of approaching academic work (Neff, Hsieh & Dejitterat 2005); and students who are higher in self-compassion are more likely to accept failures when they occur and use it as an opportunity for learning instead of sitting under their desks trying to kick passersby in fury while pulling out tufts of their own hair—that last part isn't actually in the study, but you get my drift. Self-compassionate people aim just as high as everyone else and are more likely to be resilient in the face of setbacks.

Self-Compassion Is Not Just Self-Esteem in a Different Outfit

Self-esteem is the degree to which we think of ourselves favorably in comparison to others. Self-esteem fever has gripped the world of well-being. Trundle down the bookshelves of any self-help section, and you'll find something on how to develop self-esteem so strong that not even a nuclear warhead could dent it. Unfortunately, it has some serious downsides (Neff & Vonk 2009)—it's linked to higher levels of narcissism (hilarious given that we'd more readily drink from the glass of self-esteem than self-compassion because self-compassion tastes a bit too "narcissist-y"), those who seek to maintain high levels of self-esteem might do so by engaging in downward social comparisons (sneering at people who are doing less well to make yourself feel better) and, furthermore, self-esteem is a fair-weather friend. When things are going well, self-esteem is all, "Jump in my new convertible, we'll go to the beach, you'll feel great, I even packed snacks." When things are going badly, self-esteem is all, "I'm hanging out with Jill instead, she's way more successful than you." Self-esteem is stable and a good buddy when things go well for you, and a total bully when things don't.

Self-Compassion Is Not Self-Pity

Self-pity is another societal and psychological fear. "Won't I become massively sorry for myself and walk around tripping over my bottom lip?" Self-compassion is also not besties with self-pity. Feeling self-pity is about being overwhelmed and absorbed by your own problems, a process that self-compassion researcher Kristin Neff (2003a) terms as "overidentification." People who are self-compassionate are actually more likely to face their distress with equanimity (not writhe on the floor, rending the hairshirt from their breast, wailing, "O wretched woman!" in the manner of Greek tragedy) and to step back from being overwhelmed by their suffering. That in turn allows for a broader repertoire of behaviors (self-kindness, mindfulness, connection with others) more in line with valued living, and there's no self-pity in that.

Women are particularly good at being compassionate to others but not self-compassionate. The needs of others come first. This is a one-way road to burnout. It sounds trite to say that you can't pour from an empty cup, but you actually can't. If you want the quality of your impact on yourself, loved ones, colleagues, community and the world to be sustainable, then you need sustainable self-care, something which self-compassion offers in abundance.

How to Bring Self-Compassion into Your Life

I hope that by now you feel open to the benefits of self-compassion as something to improve your life and the lives of others. Here are some ways to get started.

Find the Balance

Simply becoming aware of your emotion regulation systems and noticing when they are out of balance will do wonders for your life. You'll be able to understand what's influencing your behavior, and once you can notice this, you can step back and think about what is a helpful, value-driven behavior in any given moment rather than being a slave to your emotions.

Soothing Rhythm Breathing

When you are in threat mode, your breathing is fast and shallow. This breathing exercise (Gilbert 2009) down-regulates your threat system and turns off your stress response, allowing your soothing system to come online to generate feelings of safeness. The key thing is to get into a rhythm with your breathing here—the clue is in the name.

- Begin by finding somewhere quiet to sit, at least initially, until you are able to do this exercise in more challenging environments like trying to speak to an actual human being at your service provider when your internet is out.
- Begin by inhaling and exhaling through your nose.

- Keep your hand on your diaphragm and imagine pushing out through the stomach but keeping your shoulders where they are as you breathe out.
- Inhale for a count of four.
- Exhale for a count of four.
- Continue for at least a minute.

Once you are more skilled at this, try increasing the time to five minutes or more. The key is to breathe slowly and deeply so your physiology can slow down and send messages to your brain that all is safe.

Safe Place

Further stimulate your feelings of safety by using imagery. The beauty of imagery is that the brain responds to images in our heads in much the same way as it does to reality, even though you know the image isn't real. That means you can generate emotions not only by what you actually experience with what you see in real life, but you can generate the same emotions by creating an image in your head. This doesn't mean that you can sit in bed all day generating holiday images in the hope that you'll actually believe you are in Barbados, rather that you can create a physiologically soothing response to that image and tone down your threat system. The key here is the vividness of the images and the accompanying senses, so don't stop.

- Begin by spending a few minutes practicing soothing rhythm breathing.
- Close your eyes and imagine a place where you feel safe. It can be somewhere you have never been before or it can be somewhere you know. It can be anywhere—a beach by the ocean, a forest, a meadow, a house where you've felt very safe.
- Start by creating a vivid image of what you see around you in as much detail as possible so your brain responds to this image. Think about the light, the shadows and the colors you can see.
- Move on to focusing on what you can hear— what sounds are present? What's the loudest thing you can hear in this place? What's the quietest? Are the sounds near you or far away?
- What can you smell? The smell of the sea, the scent of fresh flowers or clean air?
- What can you feel in this place? What do you feel on your skin? What do you feel beneath your feet? Imagine taking your shoes and socks off and feeling the ground beneath your feet.
- Allow your body to relax in this place, and as you do so, bring a gentle smile to your face
- Finally, imagine that this place wants you here, that you belong here and are completely safe.

Build a Compassionate Image

To further stimulate your soothing system when you are in distress, try creating an ideal "compassionate other" (adapted from Gilbert 2009). This compassionate other may be human or it may not. It can be anything or anyone you like, and feel free to experiment to see what works with you. Frankly, I don't know what would be a nicer compassionate other than a cross between Michelle Obama, Nigella Lawson and Fozzie Bear. Whatever you choose, remember that it's your ideal and embodies what you would like from feeling soothed, cared for and cared about.

One thing before you begin. Make sure that your compassionate other has these qualities:

- **Wisdom:** it understands what it is to be human; it knows we have complex and conflicting emotions, thoughts, reactions, desires, but it can cope with all of this.
- **Strength:** it can tolerate all our distress and joy and is strong enough to protect us under any circumstances.
- **Warmth:** it has deep kindness and affection for you. Its manner is gentle and soothing.
- **Nonjudgment:** our ideal compassionate other does not condemn, judge or criticize. It accepts you as you are and is deeply committed to your well-being.

Now that you have these qualities in mind, start to build your image of your compassionate other. Here are some prompts to get you started:

- What does your compassionate other look like?
- What age would you like them to be?
- What gender?
- Do you prefer them to be human or nonhuman?
- What does your compassionate other sound like?
- What tone of voice does it use?
- Does it sound calm? Strong? Gentle?
- What smell does your compassionate other have?
- What texture does your compassionate other have? If you can imagine touching it, what would it feel like?
- How would you like your compassionate other to comfort you when you are in distress? What facial expressions does your compassionate other have as it comforts you?

Spend time developing your image in moments when you are less distressed so you can more readily call up this image to activate your soothing system when you want to tone down your threat system.

What Do I Need?

When you have slowed your system down, ask yourself these questions to guide you:

- What do I need to feel safe?
- What do I need to soothe myself?
- What do I need to feel connected?
- What do I need to step out of my mind?
- What's the kindest thing I can do for myself right now?

The tone of voice you use is important, too. Speak to yourself with gentleness, kindness and patience.

Compassionate Touch

We have evolved to be soothed by touch. It calms down our threat system and activates our soothing system. Just as a parent calms a child with touch, so you, too, can calm yourself in moments of stress with this exercise (inspired by Neff & Germer 2018). It feels odd at first, and perhaps you might practice at home before taking to rubbing your chest, or whatnot, in public spaces.

Hand-on-Heart

- When you notice you're under stress, take two to three deep breaths.

- Gently place your hand over your heart, feeling the gentle pressure and warmth of your hand. If you wish, place *both* hands on your chest, noticing the difference between one and two hands.
- Feel the touch of your hand on your chest. If you wish, you could make small circles with your hand on your chest.
- Feel the natural rising and falling of your chest as you breathe in and as you breathe out.
- Stay with the feeling for as long as you like.

If you are not into the hand-on-heart thing, you can gently stroke your arms or face, whatever works for you. Give it a go, *even though I know you are sniggering.*

Take a Break. A Self-Compassion Break

You can practice this either by bringing to mind a painful memory or by doing this in a time of emotional pain. Maybe you are caring for someone with dementia or maybe you are working in an intensive care unit—or maybe you are just having a really hard time. Try this exercise (adapted from Neff & Germer 2018) instead of eating a hundred mini Kit Kats to push away what you feel. Tell yourself:

- "Here is a moment of suffering. I am hurting. It will pass."

- "I am not alone. All human beings suffer. It is part of the human experience."

Saying this helps you realize that you have this in common with all other human beings on the planet—suffering is an unavoidable part of life. You can follow this up by putting your hands over your heart or using whatever soothing self-touch feels right to you. Other options include "Other people feel this way" or "We all struggle in our lives."

- "May I show myself kindness."

Alternatively, you can use other phrases that may apply better in your current situation, such as "May I forgive myself" or "May I be patient."

- "May I bring help and not harm."

In my view, telling yourself these things, rather than affirmations about your general amazingness and earth-shattering awesomeness, speaks much more to the reality of our shared human experience and works with, not against, how our minds operate.

Beating Burnout

I would have burned out long ago if it weren't for self-compassion. You cannot sustain a role that involves helping others—whether you are an aid worker, a parent or a paramedic—if you do not attend to your own self-care. Self-compassion goes beyond hot baths and candles to add a much more meaningful dimension to your self-care. It puts you in touch with your emotions, and therefore your own many and varied vulnerabilities, so you can keep doing what's important to you. Here's an exercise (adapted from Neff & Germer 2018) I like when things are going awry, plus you can do it "on the job" and in the moment.

- Take a few deep breaths, and bring an awareness to your feelings.
- Find a gentle rhythm with your breathing; slow your body down if you can.
- As you breathe in, imagine breathing in warmth, kindness and compassion for yourself.
- Now shift your focus to your out breath. Bring to mind someone who is suffering; that person may be in front of you, they may not.
- Breathe out warmth, kindness and compassion for that person.
- Keep breathing in compassion for you on your in breath and breathing out compassion for the other on the out breath. One for you, one for them.

This, by the way, is the psychological equivalent of putting your oxygen mask on first. You need to do something for yourself first if you are to give to others.

BOTTOM LINE

Self-compassion speaks deeply to our experience of the human condition. It offers an effective alternative to our go-to responses to distress, which are either to damp it down with short-term fixes or to engage in harsh self-criticism. Self-compassion, in contrast, encourages us to take a deep look at how we have evolved and shows us how to harness the minds we have so we can thrive. It is a profoundly different, and effective, way of transforming your relationship with yourself and others.

Chapter 9

How to Make Sense of Yourself

"It is in the character of growth that we
should learn from both pleasant and
unpleasant experiences."

—NELSON MANDELA

N ow you have some top-drawer mind mastery skills under your belt and some effective tools to make room for emotions, you can turn your mind to a deeper and more profound question: why the hell am I the way I am?

Self-Awareness or Psychological Car Maintenance

We rarely make time to invest in our self-awareness, and indeed, it feels an absurd and unnecessary luxury when there's the laundry to do (again) and school uniform to be tracked down (again). However, this is ultimately what stress is—rebounding from one demand to another without ever making time to deal with it differently because you, well, don't have time to deal with things differently. It's like having a car that doesn't run very well—it might get you to your destination, but the ride will be terrible. To improve things you have to stop and do some car maintenance if you want to cruise about enjoying your sweet ride.

Taking some time to do a little bit of self-awareness work is like your car maintenance. It will help you to make meaningful changes in your life because you'll be able to understand, and become more conscious of, how your past affects your present, and therefore your future. Being able to reflect on your life, the key moments that have shaped you, the history of your emotions and behavioral patterns offers you deep insight into what makes you tick. It is an eye-opening experience and one that can knock the wind out of you when you realize how deeply you may have been affected by past events. It is, in addition, a liberating experience. You now have the psychological tools to be able to stand back from the old, self-limiting narratives and to see your experiences in a different light, perhaps one imbued with more self-compassion. It's an opportunity to look at your past without falling into the traps of self-criticism and "shoulda, coulda, woulda" thinking, which is so much more prevalent when our minds cast only a fleeting glance backward. Taking more time to look back at the highs and lows, the joy and the suffering, the moments when you were living your values and the moments you weren't, will allow you to move forward in life with self-knowledge and self-awareness.

Throw Out a Lifeline to Yourself

The best way to structure your reflections is to do the Lifeline Exercise. It's a bit like journaling, but on steroids. There are various stages, but I am going to run you through them. I am all about exercises that can be done on the go and that don't require preparation and masses of hassle (I am, after all, supposed to be helping you with stress, not adding to your burdens) but I do think it will be of great benefit if you give yourself an hour to do this. You may need less time, that's fine, but keep an hour aside without distractions or obligations. Nothing will kill your self-awareness vibe quicker than having to empty the bins.

Creating Your Lifeline

The first thing to do is to create your lifeline. There are two ways to do this—either with a pen and paper or physically.

Pen-and-Paper Lifeline

To get started, you'll need a pen and paper. (If handy, use an 8.5 × 11-inch piece of art or construction of paper.). To begin, draw a line from one end of the paper to the other, either horizontally or vertically. This line represents your life—the start of the line is your birth and the end of the line is your life yet to come.

Starting from your birth, mark in chronological order on the line all the significant events in your life, both highs and lows. You just need to write a short note for each one. At the moment we are just getting an overview. When you get to the present day, make a short note of your hopes and dreams for the future. Turn the page for an example:

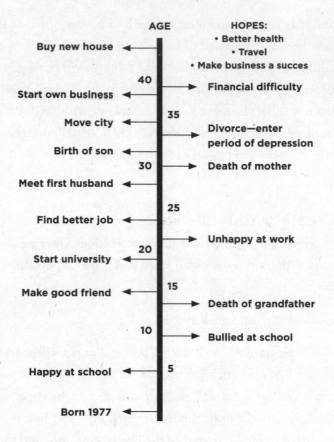

AGE

HOPES:
- Better health
- Travel
- Make business a succes

Buy new house

40

Start own business ← → Financial difficulty

35

Move city ← → Divorce—enter
period of depression

Birth of son ←

30

Meet first husband ← → Death of mother

25

Find better job ←

→ Unhappy at work

20

Start university ←

15

Make good friend ← → Death of grandfather

10

→ Bullied at school

Happy at school ← 5

Born 1977 ←

Physical Lifeline

If you prefer, you can lay out your lifeline on the floor (Schauer, Neuner & Elbert 2011). There's something about doing the lifeline in this way that does make it a deeper experience. You will need a long piece of ribbon or string (a couple of meters should do it). You will also need something to mark down significant events in your life. For the positive events you can use fake flowers, colorful beads, leaves, Haribo (depends how you feel about Haribo, I suppose), but just choose something which seems vaguely positive to you. For the difficult events, you could use stones or pebbles, dried pasta which you don't like (perhaps penne rubs you up the wrong way?) or licorice, which surely can only have negative connotations. You could even use small scrunched-up bits of paper. You will also need some Post-it notes.

. . .

Spread the ribbon out in a long line on the floor, leaving a little bit at one end scrunched up. This is to represent your life yet to come. . . . Starting at the other end, and reflecting on your life in chronological order, put down markers on the line to reflect the positive events and the difficult events. As you go, write on a Post-it note a couple of points about each event, such as when and where it happened, and stick it next to the relevant marker. Nothing too detailed, as you just want an overview at this stage. Continue marking down important events until you reach the present day. Make a short note of your hopes and dreams for the future, and place that at the end of the line. Now take a picture of your line (you might have to do this in parts—try not to get your feet in the picture unless you're wearing lovely shoes) and keep it somewhere you can get at it.

Narrating Your Lifeline

Now that you have either a drawn lifeline or a picture of your physical lifeline, you can start narrating your lifeline, event by event. I suggest you take one event at a time, in chronological order. How long you want to give each event is entirely up to you. In the interest of getting you started with a small, manageable task, limit yourself to thirty minutes and perhaps just do one event per day at the most, but it's really up to you. The idea is to write down all you can about the event. Things you may consider are:

- What was going on generally in my life at this time?
- What are the facts of this event, e.g., location, date?
- What happened?
- What feelings were present? Were these feelings I have had before or since?
- What memories are particularly vivid from this time?
- What did I learn from this event?
- What did I think about this event? Do I think about it in the same way now?
- What did I do at the time of the event?
  Were my actions helpful or harmful?
  What were the long-term and short-term consequences?
- What were my strengths at this time?

- Are there any themes or patterns I notice in my thoughts, feelings and behaviors?

Continue through each event, culminating in writing about your hopes and dreams for the future. In the end, you should have a document detailing the key events in your life. Perhaps you will have gained an insight into your emotions or maybe you have a deeper understanding of your relationships and your behaviors in them. Whatever you discover, and you will discover something useful, make a note of the times in your life when you felt you were really in tune with your values and when meaning was present. It might have been in a moment of great joy, or equally, it may have been a moment of great sadness and loss. It's often these moments that tell us what matters deeply to us. Use these insights, instead of harsh narratives your mind has come up with, to guide you through your life from now on.

Speaking Of Harsh Narratives . . .

As you take this deep dive into your past, your mind will dredge up a lot of old stories. Minds, through a prism of despair, tell stories of lives filled with regret, mistakes and missed opportunities. We are notoriously harsh narrators of our own lives and so miss opportunities to find other, new meanings from past experiences. Getting caught up in these old judgments and evaluations doesn't help, so be sure to defuse from them and do this exercise from a place of perspective and self-compassion. Similarly, some big, difficult emotions will surface—as ever, make room for them, take them with you and go about your business with kindness and understanding. These are not the narratives you are looking for. You can go about your business. Move along.

Specific Lifelines

Doing a lifeline isn't a case of one and done. You can do more detailed lifelines for specific times in your life. For example, you might want to go through your career in detail using a lifeline, or perhaps you'd like to spend more time consciously thinking about previous relationships and how they impact your life now.

One thing that can be very revealing is to do lifelines linked to particular emotions. If you have difficulties with anxiety, you can chart your history of anxiety. You can ask these questions:

- When did you first feel anxiety?
- What did you learn from your caregivers and important people in your life about anxiety?
- What significant events related to anxiety have you experienced?
- What has your relationship with anxiety been like?

- What behaviors are around when anxiety is present?

Of course, you can do this with any emotion or area of life you want to explore: health, career, money, sadness, boundaries, joy, sex, food, alcohol, work, bereavement—you name it, you can lifeline it.

BOTTOM LINE

Slowing down to take a look at what has shaped you is time well spent. Cultivating self-awareness and self-knowledge by looking at your past with your newly discovered skills will have a palpable effect on how you negotiate your future.

Chapter 10

How to Bring It All Together

ell, how was it for you? Are you feeling more psychologically flexible? Possibly even psychologically prosperous? Are you relating to your thoughts and feelings differently? Do you feel like some new avenues have opened up for you? Are you on the path of stressilience? I certainly hope so.

So, what now? I'd suggest just going back to the chapters that speak to you. When I learned about these skills, I certainly focused heavily on defusion and values to begin with. Perhaps you want to start with some values exercises before sliding over to some acceptance work? Or maybe you'd like to begin with some defusion before scooting over to some mindfulness? There's no right or wrong way to do it—leap, waltz or scuttle between any of the chapters in any order.

The most important thing is that you practice at least some of what you have read here if you actually want to change something about your life. Some of you will do that; some of you won't. Some of you will come back to it later. That's all OK. These are tools you can return to for the rest of your life. The more often you do them, the more natural they will seem to you.

I wanted this book to give you skills, but I also wanted something more: I wanted it to give you hope. Hope that, no matter where you are and what you are experiencing, there is the possibility of living a meaningful and rewarding life, a life where you can treat yourself, others and the world in a way that is important to you.

I hope that the skills you have learned here show you that you can act on your values, no matter what thoughts and feelings are running through you at any particular moment in time. You *can* control your actions. You *can* choose your values. You are so much more than just your thoughts and feelings.

This is a new way to live in your skin. Spread the word.

References

1. How to Manage Your Mind: Brain 101

p. 9 "I used to think that the human brain was the most fascinating part of the body. Then I realized, look what's telling me that." *Emo Philips, HBO Comedy Special 1987. www. youtube.com/watch?v=izH3zpAuDUs.*

2. How to Think Better

p. 21 This phenomenon was investigated by Daniel Wegner. *Wegner, Daniel M. & Schneider, David J. (2003). "The white bear story," Psychological Inquiry, 14, pp. 326–329.*

p. 27 Having Thoughts *Hayes, S. C., & Smith, S. (2005). Get Out of Your Mind and Into Your Life: The new Acceptance and Commitment Therapy. Oakland, CA: New Harbinger.*

p. 28 Thank Your Mind *Harris, R. (2008). The Happiness Trap: How to stop struggling and start living. Boston, MA: Trumpeter.*

p. 29 Singing And Funny Voices *Hayes, S. C., & Smith, S. (2005). Get Out of Your Mind and Into Your Life: The new Acceptance and Commitment Therapy. Oakland, CA: New Harbinger.*

p. 30 Over a hundred years ago, a psychologist called Edward Titchener. *Titchener, E. B. (1916). A Text-Book of Psychology. New York: Macmillan. This exercise is found in Hayes, S. C., Strosahl, K., & Wilson, K. G. (1999). Acceptance and Commitment Therapy: An experiential approach to behavior change. New York, NY: Guilford Press.*

p. 31 Carry Your Thoughts With You *Hayes, S. C., & Smith, S. (2005). Get Out of Your Mind and Into Your Life: The new Acceptance and Commitment Therapy. Oakland, CA: New Harbinger.*

p. 33 Television Screens *Harris, R. (2008). The Happiness Trap: How to stop struggling and start living. Boston, MA: Trumpeter.*

3. How to Feel Better

p. 37 "Our feelings are our most genuine paths to knowledge." *Lorde, A. (2004). Conversations with Audre Lorde. Univ. Press of Mississippi.*

p. 42 Emotions Are Actually Beach Balls *Jepsen, M., in Stoddard, J. A., & Afari, N. (2014). The Big Book of ACT*

Metaphors: A Practitioner's Guide to Experiential Exercises and Metaphors in Acceptance & Commitment Therapy. Oakland, CA: New Harbinger.

p. 52 Be the Sky *Harris, R. (2009). ACT Made Simple: An easy-to-read primer on Acceptance and Commitment Therapy. Oakland, CA: New Harbinger.*

p. 54 Urge surfing is a term coined in the 1980s by two American psychologists. *Marlatt, G.A & Gordon, J.R., eds. (1985). Relapse Prevention: Maintenance strategies in the treatment of addictive behaviors. New York: Guilford Press.*

4. How to Have Perspective

p. 59 Leaves On A Stream *Hayes, S. C., & Smith, S. (2005). Get Out of Your Mind and Into Your Life: The new Acceptance and Commitment Therapy. Oakland, CA: New Harbinger.*

p. 64 Be the Board (Steve Hayes 1999) *Hayes, S. C., Strosahl, K., & Wilson, K. G. (1999). Acceptance and Commitment Therapy: An experiential approach to behavior change. New York: Guilford Press.*

pp. 61–65 Your Thinking Self and Your Observing Self *Hayes, S. C., Strosahl, K., & Wilson, K. G. (1999). Acceptance and Commitment Therapy: An experiential approach to behavior change. New York: Guilford Press.*

p. 65 Befriending Your Observing Self (*The Continuous You* by Harris 2009) *Harris, R. (2009). ACT Made Simple: An easy-to-read* *primer on Acceptance and Commitment Therapy. Oakland, CA: New Harbinger.*

p. 66 The Continuous You *Sinclair, M., & Beadman, M. (2016). The Little ACT Workbook. Hachette, UK.*

5. How to Be Right Here, Right Now

p. 73 A Harvard study (Killingsworth & Gilbert 2010) *Killingsworth, M.A. & Gilbert, D.T, (2010). A wandering mind is an unhappy mind, Science, 12;330(6006): 932. doi: 10.1126 /science.1192439. PMID: 21071660.*

p. 77 "The awareness that arises through paying attention, on purpose, in the present moment, non-judgmentally." *Kabat-Zinn, J. (2003). Mindfulness-based interventions in context: Past, present, and future. Clinical Psychology: Science and Practice, 10(2), pp. 144–156. https://doi.org/10.1093/clipsy.bpg016.*

p. 79 Dropping An Anchor *Harris, R. (2009). ACT Made Simple: An easy-to-read primer on Acceptance and Commitment Therapy. Oakland, CA: New Harbinger.*

p. 81 Mindfulness Of Music *Hayes, S. (2019). A Liberated Mind: How to pivot toward what matters. New York: Avery.*

6. How to Live Better

p. 90 Studies looking at values. (Cohen & Sherman, 2014; Jordt, 2017) *Jordt, H., Eddy, S. L., Brazil, R., Lau, I., Mann, C.,*

References

Brownell, S. E., & Freeman, S. (2017). "Values affirmation intervention reduces achievement gap between underrepresented minority and white students in introductory biology classes." CBE— Life Sciences Education, 16(3), ar41.

p. 91 In a study by Smith et al. (2018) participants were first asked to perform a cold presser task. *Smith, B. M., Villatte, J. L., Ong, C. W., Butcher, G. M., Twohig, M. P., Levin, M. E., & Hayes, S. C. (2019). The influence of a personal values intervention on cold pressor-induced distress tolerance. Behavior Modification, 43(5), pp. 688–710.*

p. 103–104 Areas of Life (Inspired by Kelly Wilson's Valued Living Questionnaire) *Wilson, K., & Groom, J. (2006). Valued Living Questionnaire (VLQ).*

p. 105 Now We Are Eighty. Or Thirty. Or Fifty *Harris, R. (2008). The Happiness Trap: How to stop struggling and start living. Boston, MA: Trumpeter.*

p. 105 Attending Your Own Funeral *Hayes, S. C., & Smith, S. (2005). Get Out of Your Mind and Into Your Life: The New Acceptance and Commitment Therapy. Oakland, CA: New Harbinger.*

p. 108 Secret Values *Hayes, S. (2019). A Liberated Mind: How to pivot toward what matters. New York: Avery.*

p. 109 Sweet Moments (inspired by Kelly Wilson's Sweet Spot exercise, Wilson & Dufrene, 2009) *Wilson, K.G., & DuFrene, T. (2009). Mindfulness for Two: An Acceptance and Commitment*

Therapy approach to mindfulness in psychotherapy. Oakland, CA: New Harbinger.

7. How to Take Action

p. 111 "Change your life today. Don't gamble on the future, act now, without delay." *Schwarzer, A. & De Beauvoir, S. (1984). After the Second Sex: Conversations with Simone De Beauvoir. Pantheon.*

p. 113 Research shows that most people give up their New Year's resolutions by January 19. *https://www.inc.com/jeff-haden /a-study-of-800-million-activities-predictsmost-new-years -resolutions-will-be-abandoned-on-january-19-how-you-cancreate -new-habits-that-actually-stick.html, January 3, 2020.*

p. 115 Why You Keep Making the Same Mistakes *Skinner, B. F. (1953). Science and Human Behavior. New York: Macmillan.*

p. 119 Get SMART *Doran, G.T. (1981) "There's a S.M.A.R.T. way to write management's goals and objectives." Management Review, 70(11), pp. 35–36.*

p. 123 Hook Your Habits *Fogg, B. J. (2020). Tiny Habits: The Small Changes that Change Everything. Boston: Houghton Mifflin Harcourt.*

8. How to Be Self-Compassionate

p. 132 Self-compassion is made up of three distinct but interacting elements. *Neff, K. D. (2003a). "Self-compassion: An*

*alternative conceptualization of a healthy attitude toward oneself."
Self and Identity, 2(2), pp. 85–101.*

**p. 133 The first step is to understand that your brain is
basically running three types of emotional regulation systems.**
*Depue & Morrone-Strupinsky. (2005). "A neurobehavioral model of
affiliative bonding: Implications for conceptualizing a human trait
of affiliation." The Behavioral and Brain Sciences. 28, pp. 313–
350. Gilbert, P. (2009). The Compassionate Mind: A new approach
to life challenges. London: Constable and Robinson.*

p. 143 No one likes to be criticized. *Elberse, Anita "Ferguson's
Formula" Harvard Business Review https://hbr.org/2013/10
/fergusons-formula October 2013.*

**p. 143 Self-compassionate people aim just as high as those
who are not self-compassionate.** *Neff, K. D. (2003a). "Self-
Compassion: An alternative conceptualization of a healthy attitude
toward oneself." Self and Identity, 2(2), pp. 85–101.*

**p. 143 Self-compassion is also linked to adaptive ways of
approaching academic work.** *Neff, K., Hsieh, Y., & Dejitterat, K.
(2005). "Self-compassion, achievement goals, and coping with
academic failure." Self and Identity, 4, pp. 263–287.*

p. 144 Unfortunately, it has some serious downsides *Neff, K.
D., & Vonk, R. (2009). Self-compassion versus global self-esteem:
Two different ways of relating to oneself, Journal of Personality, 77,
pp. 23–50.*

References

p. 146 Soothing Rhythm Breathing *Gilbert, P. (2009). The Compassionate Mind: A new approach to life challenges. London: Constable and Robinson.*

p. 149 Build a Compassionate Image (adapted from Gilbert 2009) *Gilbert, P. (2009). The Compassionate Mind: A new approach to life challenges. London: Constable and Robinson.*

p. 151 Compassionate Touch *Neff, K. & Germer, C. (2018). The Mindful Self-Compassion Workbook: A proven way to accept yourself, build inner strength, and thrive. New York, NY: Guilford Press.*

p. 151 Have A Break. A Self-Compassion Break (adapted from Neff & Germer, 2018) *Neff, K. & Germer, C. (2018). The Mindful Self-Compassion Workbook: A proven way to accept yourself, build inner strength, and thrive. New York, NY: Guilford Press.*

p. 153 Beating Burnout (adapted from Neff & Germer, 2018) *Neff, K. & Germer, C. (2018). The Mindful Self-Compassion Workbook: A proven way to accept yourself, build inner strength, and thrive. New York, NY: Guilford Press.*

9. How to Make Sense of Yourself

p. 157 *'It is in the character of growth that we should learn from both pleasant and unpleasant experiences." Nelson Mandela at Foreign Correspondents' Association's Annual Dinner, Johannesburg, South Africa 1997.*

p. 162 Physical Lifeline *Schauer, M., Neuner, F., Elbert T. (2011). Narrative Exposure Therapy: A short-term treatment for traumatic stress disorders (2nd edition). Cambridge, MA. Hogrefe Publishing.*

Acknowledgments

I have long practiced my acknowledgments in my head. So here it goes for real: I'd like to thank the Academy for awarding me best director . . . wait! Wrong thank-you speech. Let me start again.

Firstly, a huge thank-you to my fantastic agent, Claudia Young (who is, unbeknownst to her, also working as my therapist and life coach), and all at Greene & Heaton—you have seen me through my first book seamlessly and calmly. I am truly grateful.

To my editor at Fourth Estate, Michelle Kane—I knew when I first met you that you were the editor for me; you had me at "Do you have your security pass?" Just as well you thought I was an author for you. Thanks so much for your humor and encouragement, and to all at Fourth Estate for getting behind *Stressilient* in the way that you have. And a special thank-you to Annie Ridout, who kindly introduced us in the first place.

As always, my family have been tremendous sources of support, and there are many of you to thank, so here goes—thank

Acknowledgments

you to my husband Nick for your love, encouragement and incomparable Yorkshire puddings. To Sophia, my unique daughter—you light up my life every single day; I thought I was here to teach you, but now I think it might be the other way 'round. I am so proud of your creativity, kindness and humor. And, of course, to the ever-loyal and loving S, for a lifetime of comfort—you know who you are. To Sara Hossain and David Bergman, for always being on hand with hugs, dinners and making me chop vegetables. To all my extended family and in-laws—there are too many of you to name individually, and I am too scared to try lest I forget anyone, but I am grateful to all of you. There, that should keep me out of trouble.

Now for the friends. Jill Dickerson, Dina Hossain (a cousin lurking among the friends) and Claudia Bellini—you are my soulmates, and I am truly lucky to have you in my corner. Henny Finch, Charlotte Bigland and James Coleman—you have offered friendship and solid shoulders to lean on for over twenty-five years. You are the best triumvirate outside of ancient Rome. Esther Kelbert—thank you for walking me up and down the river by Hammersmith countless times, a bit like a dog. You are the best listener I know.

My deepest gratitude to Kerry Young and Millay Vann for their humor, wisdom and teaching me just about everything I know about trauma. Thank you for letting me be me. I don't know what I would do without you two. Really. Now, please stop touching my stuff.

Thank you also to the ACT community, but particularly to Joe Oliver—you have always been so generous with your time and knowledge, not least by reading chapters from this book and

Acknowledgments

either not being annoyed by my emails or being too polite to say so. And, of course, my thanks and gratitude to all the patients I have seen over the years who have shared their journeys with me. I hope I have been of some help.

There are three people without whom I would never have written this book (so if you don't like it, blame them). Larushka Ivan-Zadeh—thank you for your unfaltering encouragement and patient proofreading. To be supported by a writer of your caliber is an amazing vote of confidence. Adele Stevens—you kept me going right from the start. Thank you for always getting me out of my own way when I am being my own worst enemy. You are the expert in that. Nicky Yates—many years ago you said I should write something, so I did, and now look! Thank you not only for getting me started, but for your ongoing positivity, enthusiasm and style advice.

Finally, I can't adequately express enough gratitude to my wonderful parents. Everything I am and any good that I might do, I owe to you. Thank you, Dad, for being my rock, for your compassion and for your unconditional love. And, of course, to my much-missed and much-adored mother, thank you for showing me what was possible. I know you are with me, always.

SAM AKBAR, Ph.D., is a London-based psychologist specializing in patients who have survived serious trauma (war, torture, sexual violence). She also trains psychologists, who in turn have treated trauma victims around the world, including in trauma hot spots, such as refugee camps in Iraq. Akbar is an Oxford University graduate with a doctorate in clinical psychology from University College, London.